CON

THINGS INDIANA JONES AND THE GREAT CIRCLE

ESSENTIAL TIPS AND TRICKS

EXPLORATION TIPS

Exploration is a huge part of Indiana Jones and the Great Circle – even moreso than combat. After some early tutorials and arriving in the Vatican City, you'll be ushered around to complete your main objectives, but you're also free to run around and explore at your leisure. This means you can search around for photo ops, find Adventure Books to level Indy up, discover notes to earn adventure points, etc.

Side-quests are called Fieldwork in this game, and you won't just find dozens of exclamation marks on your map to start them. To begin a Fieldwork quest, you'll need to find some sort of note that unlocks it. For example, an early main story quest has you taking pictures of inscriptions scattered around the Vatican, of which you only need four. Once you turn in this quest, Antonio, the NPC who assigned it to you, will suggest that you find six more for him. And so, while the main quest will continue the story, this job gets added to your Fieldwork tab. Another not-so-obvious example is you might come across a seemingly random note. The note may mention that a child has been locked up for stealing artifacts. There might be more to the story, and thus, a Fieldwork is added to your journal for Indy to investigate.

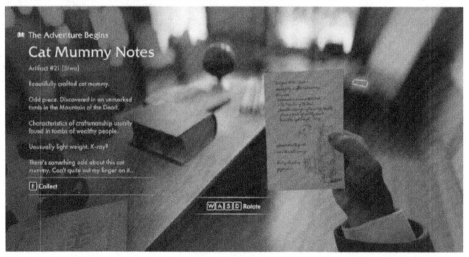

Leveling is a bit different than what you might be used to compared to other games of this style. Indy will level by discovering and looting things in the world. First, Adventure Books are the key to powering up Indy. There's no leveling system or skill trees. Instead, you'll find an Adventure Book that, for example, lets you hit harder. To unlock this skill though, you'll need to spend adventure points, money, or medicine bottles, which all come from exploring and looting everything you find in the world.

4

Once you have bought a camera, be sure to keep an eye out for the camera symbol on the top left of your screen. If you see it pop up, that means there is something to take a picture of, which will net you adventure points as a photo op!

While the big, bright open streets of the Vatican are nice to stroll around, you will often find yourself delving into dark crypts. You'll get a lighter later on, but starting out, you'll need to manage keeping a torch around. First off, make sure to light every brazier you find. Not only do they provide a source of light and a breadcrumb trail to track where you've been, but they can re-light any torches you find just in case you lose yours.

If you lose your torch, you can oftentimes find jars of unlit torches for you to grab, or sometimes you can find them on the walls.

Another big hurdle is that Indy will drop his torch when performing various actions. For example, if you need to swing over a gap or climb up on a ledge, once you extend the whip, he'll drop the torch. To counter this, aim and throw your torch to where you're headed. That way you can swing across or climb up, and then snag your torch off the ground.

You can throw your torch through gaps in walls, as well. An early puzzle you'll find has you squeezing through a gap in the wall, only for water to extinguish your flame. When things like this happen, it's very likely that the room has a window for you to toss your torch through. Furthermore, try to avoid using the torch to bash enemies, as it'll break, and you'll be without your light source. Instead, drop it and either use your fists, whip their weapon out of their hand, or just find something else lying around. Once the combat is over, pick up your torch.

Climbing takes stamina, so make sure Indy is rested before trying to make it up a big wall. Luckily, it only drains when you move, so you can always stop moving to rest and recover.

Give yourself an extra boost of stamina by eating a piece of fruit. Fruit will give you a bonus to your stamina, while bread gives you a bonus to your health.

White chalk, paint, and scuff marks is your cue on where you can traverse. If you see a ledge or a door covered with white chalk, that typically means you can climb or interact with it in some way.

You will occasionally come across lockboxes with either a lock or a combination. If it requires a combination, look for a nearby note or just something to interact with around the lock, as the code is typically nearby.

If you need to know where to go for your currently tracked quest, bring up your map. Not only will it show you on the map where to go, but it'll also create a waypoint out in the world for you to follow. You can go into your exploration difficulty settings and set it to always show the waypoint if you'd like.

STEALTH TIPS

As previously mentioned, stealth is your friend in the Great Circle, as there aren't a lot of reasons to fight. So let's first go over a few ways to slink your way through the game.

Early on, enemy AI is fairly typical. An enemy will spot you, and if the circle above their head fills up, they'll yell out and alert everyone around them. You can use this to your advantage by having them spot you and luring them around corners to knock them out.

You can also sneak up on enemies with a melee weapon in hand and knock them out that way as well. Just make sure to hide the body as other patrolling enemies can find it and will start screaming.

Indy has a lean function that is quite useful when peering around corners. As long as you have something in your hand, you can hold the left trigger and then click on the left or right stick to lean. This allows you to see around corners while remaining hidden.

If you do get busted in the city, either by doing something like cracking your whip too close to people, or hanging around near a guard who can see through your disguise, it's best to run away and hide. It takes a while, but if you break the enemy's line of sight, the flashing circle around your health bar will eventually stop pulsing, allowing you to once again become incognito.

COMBAT TIPS

Everything is a weapon in Indiana Jones and the Great Circle. And when I say everything, I mean, most things. Littered around combat zones will be various one-handed and two-handed weapons for Indy to pick up and use. Improvised Weapons play a huge part in this game's combat, so these tips will prove useful:

Anything you find can be thrown, be it to distract guards so you can sneak around, or heck, even to throw a hammer at a man's face. But once you're in smacking range, it's never long before the item crumbles to dust. So always be on the lookout for things to pick up.

A few early disguises, like the Clerical Suit and the Blackshirt Uniform, come with a weapon in your satchel that never goes away. It can still break, but you can use a repair kit to fix it. Just know that repair kits are few and far between, and your weapon will break constantly, so use these sparingly to knock out a guard if there's nothing else around.

Indy also carries his famous revolver. The revolver is deadly, but I'd recommend against using it much. Ammo is incredibly sparse, and shooting the gun will alert everyone within the vicinity. I'd say that you should only use it if you have no other option – everyone is already alerted, and you just need to quickly thin out the herd of enemies.

Combat in this game can be slapstick levels of fun, it's all about using the environment to your advantage. You can dodge around while fighting, and parry to block and launch counterattacks at foes.

Early on, most of the fights will play out in the fashion of you whipping an enemy, which stuns them and makes them drop their weapon, only for you to then pick it up and use it against them. Again, you can throw your weapon at an enemy for a fun ranged attack, but unless they're stunned, they're really good at dodging them. Heck, if they're on full alert, they can even catch the weapon.

The gamut of enemies early on ranges from scrawny little dudes to big muscle boys to even healers. For the scrawny dudes, just knock them out, they're weak. For the muscle guys, they'll block a lot of your attacks. Hold the attack button, which consumes a bar of stamina, to give them a hard thwack to break their guard. Then trade blows with them, mixing in dodges and parries.

Be mindful that everything you do costs stamina, so don't just go crazy with your attacks and dodges. Running out of stamina will blur your screen and massively slow down your punches and dodges, and we don't want that.

There are also healer enemies adorned with green crosses. These guys fight like a heavy and almost always drop a bandage when they're taken out. And watch out, if you let them linger too long, they could resurrect one of your fallen enemies.

HOW_TO'S GUIDE

HOW TO GET THE CAMERA

How To Get To The Vatican Post Office

After you emerge from the catacombs in the library, Antonio will give you the Clerical Key. This lets you open doors with stained-glass windows throughout Vatican City, including those that lead to the stairwell out of the library. Use it to reach the streets outside.

You'll emerge in Belvedere Plaza. Note the military tents on the left; there are some items inside that you can steal, including money that will be useful later, but you need to do so without being seen. See below for tips on stealing from the fascists.

The road to the Vatican Post Office is through the tunnel between the two tents. At the other end, you'll find that the street is blocked off by soldiers, and the clergy are arguing with the guards. Even if you were to fight the soldiers (which is not recommended), the gate would still be closed and locked; you need to find another way around.

Facing the locked gate, look to the right; there's an alleyway that you can enter. Use the crates to climb onto the nearby roof and make your way over the gate. You can zipline back to the street level using the rope on the far side.

How To Get Inside The Vatican Post Office

The street around the Vatican Post Office is a restricted area until the soldiers leave; even if with your disguise, guards will attack if they see you. Your zipline escapade may have alerted a lone guard, who will investigate your landing spot; listen for his dialogue, and take him down stealthily with a nearby object if you have to.

If you do have to knock out the guard, immediately pick him up and hide him behind the truck in the corner; another guard patrols this area with a dog and will see the body if you don't.

Stay out of sight until the guard with the dog turns to leave, then climb into the open window at the rear of the Post Office, indicated by a flowing white curtain.

How To Get Enough Money To Buy The Camera

Take the Risotto Recipe from the table across from the window, then use the Clerical Key to enter the main area of the Post Office through the door to your right. Speak to Ernesto in his office, and he'll demand 379 lire for the camera.

Tip: The soldiers leave the area during the conversation with Ernesto, so you can now come and go through the front door and use the previously-closed street to easily return to Belvedere Plaza.

If you don't have enough cash, the easiest way to get it is to return to the military tents on the plaza and steal it. The tent closest to the library is lightly guarded; as long as nobody else is inside, you should have little trouble getting away with your petty crime.

Warning: If you do get caught stealing, run away and get to another area; a fight here will bring the entire army down on your head.

The other tent is trickier, as it's watched by the Blackshirt in the guard booth next to the tunnel. The easiest method for handling him is to take the cleaning brush from the bucket in the tent by the library, or some other innocent-looking tool, and wait by the guard booth until nobody is looking. When the coast is clear, knock out the guard and quickly walk into the tent and swipe the cash before anyone notices.

Tip: Be sure to take the Medicine Bottle from the table as well; you can use it to trade for Adventure Books with Sister Valeria, who runs the Pharmacy near the Post Office.

❖ *How To Open The Locked Chest*

On the far side of the tent is a chest secured by a combination lock. You can find the combination in the drawer of the desk next to it. The movie ticket in the drawer is partially punched; by turning it over, you can find the first half of the combination. The code is 5238.

The chest has a wad of bills inside, which will go a long way toward purchasing the camera.

❖ *How To Buy The Camera From Ernesto*

When you have the money, pick up the camera from Ernesto's desk and use the jump button to confirm the purchase. If you have extra money left over, you can buy the Adventure Books on the right side of the desk using the same method.

HOW TO REGAIN AND INCREASE STAMINA

How to Regain Stamina

Indiana Jones and the Great Circle allows players to replenish their stamina in various ways. Every time you punch, melee strike, sprint, and jump, your stamina block decreases, and you'll need to get it back up before engaging in another cardio workout. Here are all the ways players can regain/replenish their stamina in Indiana Jones and the Great Circle:

- Take a breather: The game allows Indy to regenerate his stamina bar. However, you'll have to take a short break from all stamina-consuming actions to replenish the bar. It's a slow process that can get quicker as you upgrade your character.

- Stamina Recovery Moves: Players can upgrade their skills and unlock special ones through various books found around the world. There are some combat moves like Punch Out, which allows Indy to recover some stamina after knocking out an enemy. It's a great skill to acquire if you're trapped in a corner with multiple enemies.

How to Increase Max Stamina

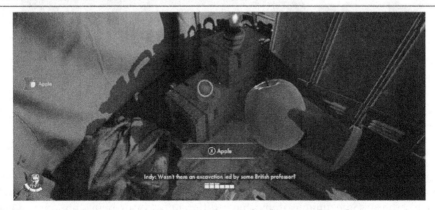

Similar to regaining stamina, there are also multiple ways that players can increase their maximum stamina in Indiana Jones and the Great Circle. However, one method helps you temporarily increase Indy's maximum stamina, while the other increases it permanently. Let's check out both of the methods.

- Eating Fruits: Players can find different varieties of food, like fruits and snacks, scattered around different locations. Consuming fruits like apples or lemons will give Indy an extra bar of stamina on top of normal ones. However, once this bar is consumed, you'll have to eat more fruit to regain it.

- Purchasing "Moxie" Fitness Books: In addition to skill-unlocking books, players can also purchase books that can increase maximum stamina permanently. These books are called "Fitness Moxie" and can be found at stalls. Once purchased, players will increase their total stamina considerably. Purchasing the next installment of said book, Moxie II and Moxie III, will further increase maximum stamina.

HOW TO CHANGE OUTFITS

How to Claim Outfits

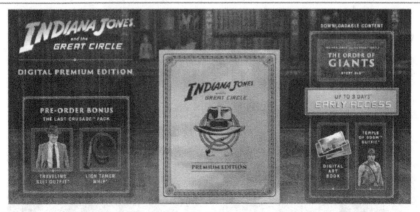

To claim outfits, players will need to either head to the Steam Page or the Xbox Store of Indiana Jones and the Great Circle. From here, they can find the Add-ons/DLC section, where some unique items have different ways of being obtained. Once claimed, the outfit will automatically unlock in-game:

- Traveling Suit Outfit – Pre-Order Indiana Jones and the Great Circle or Purchase the Digital Premium Upgrade

- Lion Tamer Whip – Pre-Order Indiana Jones and the Great Circle or Purchase the Digital Premium Upgrade

- Temple of Doom Outfit – Purchase the Digital Premium Upgrade

How to Change Outfits

Once players have a selection of outfits, they can head into the Options Menu in-game through the start button, and at the very bottom of the Hud & Gameplay Options page, they will find the menu for Special Outfits, which allows them to seamlessly select between their Outfit with the d-pad, or their Whip, also with the D-Pad.

Indiana Jones' outfit will change seamlessly, allowing players to wear the iconic garb of their favorite archeologist's adventures, to be seen in cutscenes, during third-person gameplay segments, or whenever they look down to marvel at Indy's attire from a first-person perspective.

HOW TO FAST TRAVEL

While exploring a location, players will come across sign boards with the names of locations marked on them. Moving your cursor over the name of a location will give you the option of fast traveling to the selected location. Once the players confirm, after a brief loading time depending on your system's performance, they'll fast-travel to the selected location within the map.

It's an infinite-use mechanic that doesn't require any special resources or currency. However, there are a few limitations to using fast travel in Indiana Jones and the Great Circle.

- Players can only fast-travel to a location they've visited before.

- Players cannot travel to every location on a map with fast travel, only specific ones with a sign board.

- Players cannot fast-travel while in combat status.
- Players cannot fast-travel to other maps, only locations within a map in Indiana Jones and the Great Circle.

HOW TO GET MAP HINTS

How to Spend Money

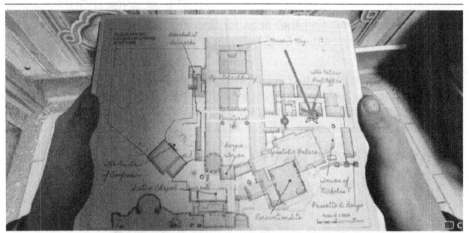

On Indy's travels, he might come across a bought of coins and bills to stash his pockets with the currency of the country he is in. If players are in the Vatican, then they might have found plenty of currency, but without an understanding of what to do with them. Luckily, there is a point to money in Indiana Jones and the Great Circle, and players should try to get their hands on as much as it as they can. After players reach the Vatican and talk to Antonio in his office, Indiana Jones will be instructed to go to the Vatican Post Office, found on the East side of the map.

Inside the Vatican Post Office, players can find the janitor, Ernesto, who will offer a few useful items to Indiana Jones in exchange for a rather extortionate amount of money. Players must first purchase the Camera from Ernesto, which will cost around 350 Lira. After that, players can return to Ernesto to purchase a bundle of useful items by interacting with them on his desk:

- Vatican Artifacts (300 Lira) – Shows all locations of lost artifacts in the Vatican
- Vatican Books (300 Lira) – Shows all locations of adventure books in the Vatican
- Vatican Mysteries (300 Lira) – Shows all locations of Mysteries in the Vatican
- Vatican Notes (600 Lira) – Shows all locations of notes in the Vatican

Each one of these items purchased will reveal new discoverable items and quests on the Vatican map.

16

HOW TO USE REPAIR KITS

How To Get Repair Kits

Right from the early quests and locations in the game, you'll encounter Repair Kits. They'll be lying on the ground and can be picked up by press X. They look like little grey boxes and they'll usually be found propped up against benches and boxes in enemy camps.

Once you've found them, they'll be added to your inventory to be used at any time. However, you can only carry a maximum of ten Repair Kits at any one time.

How To Use Repair Kits

However, using the Repair Kits you have is trickier because the game never explains it. Once you've broken one of your weapons, it will show as snapped in half in its icon on the left of the screen.

You can only break your weapon when using it as a melee weapon, and not when shooting if it's a gun.

With the weapon broken and equipped, press right on the d-pad to open the inventory. Then, press left to select the weapon you're using. You should then be able to hold X to repair it using one of the Repair Kits in your inventory. You'll then be able to use it as normal once more.

If you've found multiple disguises in a location, you'll have different default weapons you can use. Simply select the disguise to see the weapon, as they may also be broken.

HOW TO GET THE LIGHTER

How To Get The Lighter

Once you first arrive in Gizeh and meet Nawal, she asks you to head out into the blazing Egyptian heat to find four stone Stele, while helping her in the mystery of the Great Circle. We won't want to spoil what happens once you've found them all.

Finding the four Stele is now your main objective, so you can head to four locations that are indicated on your map. However, you'll run into issues at three of those locations.

They are tunnels underneath the surface in Gizeh, and therefore dark and sometimes filled with scorpions. You need to light the way to see where the Stele are.

To get the Lighter, head to the town area north of where you started in Gizeh, where the objective marker is. There, you'll meet Asmaa, who'll give the Lighter to you for a small fee. If you want them, she'll also sell some books to you which show the location of all Books in the region, as well as where to start all Mysteries.

Be sure to take a picture of Asmaa for some quick Adventure Points.

How To Use The Lighter

Once you have the Lighter, you can head back to the locations of the Stele. There, you'll need to equip the Lighter by pressing up on the d-pad. It will light automatically, but you can light more of the space around you by holding the left trigger on your controller.

Then, with it lit, you can wave it near candles, bowls of fuel, or torches to light them with the Lighter, allowing you to see in dark spaces without having to equip the item at all times.

You can burn away red posters you spot throughout the game by using the Lighter. You get 50 Adventure Points for each one you light.

BEGINNER TIPS

TAKE YOUR TIME

Great Circle is meant to be played at whatever pace suits you. If you want to just rush through objectives and complete the main story you certainly can, but there's no time limit. If you're the kind of player who likes to explore every corner and search for collectibles, this is one for you.

Don't hesitate to take it slow and get to know each of the game's areas. You'll be glad you did; in almost every case, you'll be rewarded with extra items, new skills, or side quests that you wouldn't have found if you'd stuck to the straight and narrow path.

MYSTERIES HAVE ALL THEIR CLUES NEARBY

There are dozens of quick puzzles called Mysteries hidden throughout the game. Most can be solved in a few minutes, assuming that you find all the necessary clues, and offer worthwhile rewards.

Unlike some of the larger quests, Mysteries all have the hints that you need to solve them in the same room or area. If you find one Mystery Note, there will be others nearby; look for drawers, cupboards, or hidden objects if something still doesn't add up.

AVOID UNNECESSARY FIGHTS

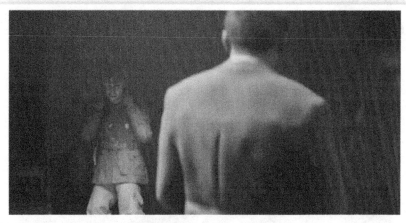

While punching Nazis is certainly a high point of any Indiana Jones adventure, and you'll get to do plenty of it throughout the game, rushing into combat rarely ends well. Indy can take maybe two bad guys in a fistfight at most; any more than that, and you're going to need some melee weapons or your trusty revolver to even the odds, or run away.

Stealth is always preferable when you can manage it, since enemies catching you and calling for reinforcements usually means you're about to load a checkpoint whether you like it or not. There's no bonus for beating enemies either, and since you're bound to take a little bit of damage in any scuffle, starting fights is usually a net negative.

MOST AREAS HAVE MULTIPLE ROUTES

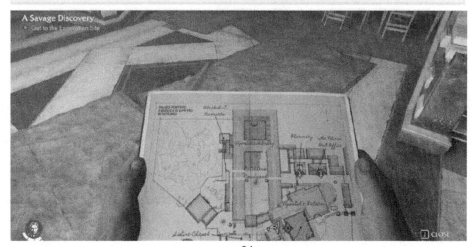

Each open-world area in the game is designed so that you can get anywhere from anywhere else, though some routes might take a little more ingenuity than others. Whatever your current objective, there's going to be more than one way to get there.

If the shortest or most obvious route is crawling with guards, try looking for a rooftop path or a side entrance. They won't always be obvious, but once you find the area map you can usually extrapolate and improvise.

"STEAL" MEANS YOU'LL GET CAUGHT

Even if your current disguise lets you get into an otherwise-restricted area, you can't just take everything that's nailed down. Enemies that see you swiping their cash, supplies, and important documents will attack. If the pickup indicator for an item is red, and the action reads that you'd be stealing the item, it means an enemy is watching you.

Once the enemy no longer has you in their line of sight, targeting the item again should turn the indicator the normal white color and remove the steal descriptor. It's only stealing if you get caught!

TAKE PICTURES AT EVERY OPPORTUNITY

Early in the game, you'll get yourself a camera that you can use to take pictures of scenery, people, and objects that you encounter. It's required for some quests, but you can also take pictures for additional Adventure Points, which can be spent on new Skills.

If you hear a shutter click and the camera icon appears on the left side of the screen, a photo opportunity is nearby.

Be sure to take every possible photo opportunity you come across. The extra AP adds up quickly, and some photos can be given to NPCs for even more Adventure Points.

IF YOU'RE STUCK, LOOK UP

There aren't many true dead ends in Indiana Jones And The Great Circle. If the way forward is blocked, or doesn't seem to exist at all, there's a good chance that you're expected to climb something. Look for places that you can swing or grapple with the whip, or ledges that you can jump to.

White sheets, paint, and curtains are used to indicate spots where Indy can climb or swing.

INSPECT EVERYTHING

This is the kind of game where, outside of a handful of red herrings, if an object can be interacted with, it's going to be important somehow or other. Rotate objects to look for hidden symbols, check the back of every sheet of paper that you find, and check every door to see if it opens.

While Indy's Journal does a passable job of tracking all the information that you find it can be a little clunky to use. It can be worth having a notes app or a pen and paper nearby to jot things down so that you don't have to keep flipping through the journal.

COMBAT TIPS

USE THE WHIP OFTEN

It should come as no surprise that Indy's signature weapon is one of your best assets in a fight. The whip doesn't do any real damage, but it has two main uses in combat that give you a huge advantage, especially in one-on-one brawls:

- A short press of the whip button lets you crack the whip at a foe, causing them to flinch and possibly drop their weapon.

- A long press of the whip button lets you wrap the whip around an enemy's limb, then press the button again to pull them toward you. Catching their leg will knock them to the ground, while catching their arm pulls them in for a grapple, letting you punch them repeatedly before they break free.

The whip also has a considerably long range, more than enough for most fights. All in all, it's your biggest consistent advantage over your foes - use it!

Warning: Trying to grab heavy enemies with the whip will cause them to pull you instead.

SAVE AMMO FOR BOSSES AND EMERGENCIES

Revolver bullets are among the rarest resources in the entire game. When you do find any extras, they will be in very small quantities, usually two. This means you need to save your ammo for when you really need it.

The best time to break out the revolver is against bosses, who can take a lot of damage no matter the source. Filling them with a few slugs will help put the momentum of the fight in your favor, which you'll need; most bosses only need to get a couple good hits to take you out.

The other time to use bullets is at the end of a prolonged fight where you don't want to risk restarting the whole encounter. If wasting a shot or two means the last foe doesn't send you back to a checkpoint, it's usually worth it.

Tip: If an enemy drops a gun, you can always use that one instead of using up your own bullets.

STAY WELL-FED

PACKING
Fruit Bag
Carry twice the amount of fruit.
Adventure Points To Unlock: 250
[E] Collect

Archeology is hungry work, especially when it involves dramatic fist-fights in exotic locales. Food boosts Indy's stats above their normal maximum, so you should munch on anything you find, especially if you're in a heavily-guarded area.

- Bread increases the maximum damage that one section of Indy's health bar can take before being removed. As long as a bar isn't fully depleted, it will regenerate without needing to apply a Bandage.

- Fruit gives Indy extra Stamina, letting you block, dodge, and charge power punches longer without having to recuperate.

Warning: Each food item is a one-time boost, so once the benefit is exhausted you'll need to eat again to get it back.

Until you get some upgrades via Adventure Books, your carrying capacity for both food types is very limited. If you find food that would put you over your limit, eat what you already have to make room. The only reason not to do this is if you're fully maxed out on Health or Stamina, which is a very rare occurrence.

PC PLAYERS: USE A CONTROLLER

If you're playing Indiana Jones And The Great Circle on PC, do yourself a favor and switch to a controller instead of using the mouse and keyboard setup. The game's fistfighting mechanics were built with controllers in mind, and using a mouse is going to trip you up in a way that changing the keybinds won't fix.

As per the usual setup, RMB is for aiming and LMB is for throwing and shooting. So far, so normal. The trouble, though, is that in melee combat, RMB throws a punch with Indy's left hand, and LMB throws a punch with his right. This makes countering after a block hard to manage, as you're more likely to push your opponent away than to sock him if you go with your split-second reaction.

Switching to a controller, where the left and right shoulder buttons are mapped to the corresponding hands, fixes the problem.

DEAL WITH DOGS FIRST

Many of the secure areas you'll be infiltrating have guard dogs in addition to human guards. Dogs can grapple Indy for several seconds, dealing damage as you struggle to get them off of you; it's best to remove them from the picture first.

Don't worry, you don't have to shoot the dogs. They're frightened by loud noises, so a whip crack or gunshot near them is usually enough to get them to leave. At that point, you can turn your attention to the humans.

WATCH YOUR BACK

Since the game is in first-person, it can be tough to keep track of everything that's going on around you. That's doubly true in combat, especially if there are multiple enemies to contend with. Even if you think you have a fight well-in-hand, all it takes is for one bad guy to sneak up behind you for things to go south.

If you can, fight with your back to a wall, but away from a corner. This prevents an enemy from getting the drop on you, but still leaves you with an opening to dodge to the left or right as needed. If you have to fight in the open, keep moving and dodging so that you can look around, and keep track of how many enemies are still standing.

Until there are just one or two foes that can be easily accounted for, stick to quick one-two jabs to wear enemies down, rather than prolonged combos that can leave you in one place and therefore vulnerable.

KNOW WHERE MELEE WEAPONS ARE

Most areas have several melee weapons strewn about for you to pick up and use. They won't last more than a few strikes, but they deal incredible damage compared to your fists. Grabbing one mid-fight is a sure way to gain the upper hand.

If a particular battle is giving you trouble, make note of any weapons that you can use on your next attempt. Going straight for them and using them to thin enemy numbers quickly goes a long way toward turning a losing fight into a winning one.

DISCRETION IS THE BETTER PART OF VALOR

Except for bosses and a few scripted encounters, nearly every fight in the game is completely optional. Throwing items to distract guards, picking bad guys off one by one, or just sneaking on past without anybody noticing will all save you the trouble and the resources of committing to a fight.

By the same token, there's no shame in running away if your health gets low. If a fight is stacked against you, there's no reason to stick around if fleeing is an option; you won't get any extra reward for single-handedly taking down a full squad, besides bragging rights.

THINGS INDIANA JONES AND THE GREAT CIRCLE DOESN'T TELL YOU

SOME WEAPONS ARE MORE DURABLE THAN OTHERS

As you arrive in The Vatican, you'll soon learn to love Improvised Weapons: random objects lying about that Indy can grab and clobber some unsuspecting fascist from behind with. Many of these weapons will break immediately after performing a silent takedown, but that's not always the case.

When you pick up a weapon, note the amount of dots that appear in the bottom right corner of the screen. This is the weapon's durability, and indicates how much you can use it before it breaks apart. Knocking an enemy out from behind usually takes around 3 points of durability, but can still work if you use, say, a flyswatter that only has a single point.

You can also sometimes find heavier, bigger weapons, like metal pipes or maces that can take out multiple unaware foes, or last in direct combat for far longer before going to pieces, so don't be afraid to swap what you're holding.

YOU CAN REPAIR SOME WEAPONS

In certain areas, you can sometimes find Repair Kits, but using them isn't all that intuitive. Since most weapons break after only a few uses, it may not be readily apparent how to make use of these kits.

In fact, the only weapons you can use Repair Kits on, are weapons that come with certain disguises. Your Clerical Suit for example has its own staff weapon that you can equip at any time if you're short on finding an Improvised Weapon. Unlike other weapons, your disguise weapons remain in your inventory even after being broken, which is where Repair Kits come into play.

With the ability to repair the weapon attached to your disguise, you can think of it as always having a backup weapon at the ready if you find yourself in a location where Improvised Weapons are hard to come by, or need to take out multiple enemies from behind in quick succession.

THERE ARE MULTIPLE WAYS TO REACH OBJECTIVES

It goes without saying, but exploration is a huge part of Indiana Jones and the Great Circle. Because of this, you may find that there are multiple ways to approach many of you objectives in the semi-open world areas.

If certain areas are highly guarded, don't be afraid to look around for other paths. Pay attention to bars on ledges you can grab onto, or poles you can swing from to bypass hostile areas. You can also stop swinging to climb straight up instead of only swinging across.

Other areas, like the Apostolic Palace, have multiple entrances and exits, and some can be unlocked by undertaking certain side quests that let you gain access to different wings of the palace that may otherwise be locked to you.

BEATING UP BAD GUYS DOESN'T GIVE XP

Unlike many games, there's actually not too many benefits from beating up the bad guys, other than clearing a path to your objective, or grabbing whatever weapon they may be holding. Enemies don't drop loot or money, and you can't gain experience or levels by taking on a barracks full of fascists.

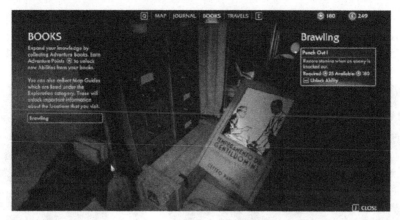

Instead, the way you increase your skills is by finding Adventure Books stashed around the world, and use Adventure Points to unlock the skills within these books. Adventure Points are given by finding a variety of collectibles like Notes and Discoveries, or by solving Mysteries and completing Fieldwork Sidequests.

It really pays to be observant and explore as much as you can, as even the most innocuous note you collect can help you unlock that next skill.

NOTES CAN TRIGGER QUESTS AND MYSTERIES

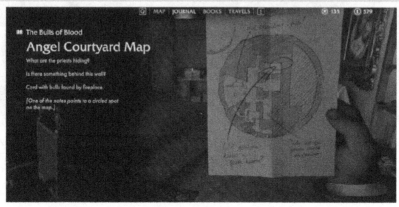

You won't find giant exclamation marks while wandering around the Vatican or Gizeh in your adventure, but there are quests to undertake. However, many of these can be started by finding an associated note that will clue Indy in on a lead.

Certain times, finding a note or flyer from someone will start a Fieldwork Sidequest and let you know who you can talk to to properly start a side quest. Other times, you may find there's a mysterious puzzle nearby, but reading a note in the room will trigger the Mystery in your journal. If you see something marked "Mystery Note" there's a good chance there's a puzzle somewhere in the room that needs solving!

FINDING MEDICINE CAN HELP INCREASE YOUR HEALTH

In each major region, you can come across Medicine Bottles stolen away by nazis or fascists. There are characters in each locale who need this medicine, and are willing to trade in exchange for unique Adventure Books.

These books are the only way you can increase Indy's health and stamina beyond its initial value, so always be on the lookout for these medicine bottles, especially when in territory occupied by bad guys!

YOU CAN BREAK OPEN TREASURE BOXES

While plundering fascist or nazi outposts of their money, it's easy to overlook the most lucrative objects you can find.

When in designated enemy territory like tents, camps, or officer barracks, be sure to look around for small boxes that are padlocked (your reticle will turn from white to red when moving over them). It may not seem like you can do anything to them — at least not with your fists — but an Improvised Weapon can actually break the lock and reveal currency inside!

You can also simply shoot the lock off with your trusty revolver, but be absolutely sure no bad guys are still around nearby or they will come running!

SECRET INTERACTIONS

While this game's side quests are a bit more involved than doing mindless busywork for random citizens, there are ways you can help out average people with tasks and get rewarded for it. These little interactions aren't marked in your journal or identified in any way — you just need to keep an eye out for someone in need.

If you ever walk past a person complaining about something: a book out of reach, a missing tool, or even lamenting they don't have a photo of something or something, you might actually be able to help! Look around nearby to see if you can spot the object they need, and then bring it over. You can usually place the item on a table nearby, and doing so will reward you with a few extra Adventure Points!

DOS AND DON'TS OF DISGUISES

A lot of Indiana Jones' adventure will rely on using disguises to blend in with the locals while you hunt down clues, and it's worth knowing what you can and can't get away with while using these disguises.

- Guards won't hassle you if you're wearing the right disguise for an area, but Captains can slowly spot out that you are a fake, regardless of which disguise you wear.

- Guards WILL get mad if you get too out of character. This means using your whip, even to climb or swing on something.

- However, climbing ladders, or vaulting up ledges, even scaffolding won't attract attention. Civilians won't really care if you do use your whip for things, and so long as guards aren't nearby, nobody will be alerted.

- If you notice an eye icon next to Indy's portrait, it means you're being watched by guards. Grabbing things like money or similar items will say "steal" and indicate that you will be attacked if you follow through with the action.

- If you wait until they are no longer looking, or distract guards with thrown bottles, the eye icon will disappear along with the "steal" notification, meaning you are clear to grab the items without repercussion.

SOME DISGUISES CAN TRIVIALIZE RESTRICTED AREAS

Early in your adventure you can gain a Clerical Suit Disguise to blend in while in the Vatican City, but that won't stop Blackshirts from attacking you on sight if you step into their military zones.

The good news is there are certain other disguises that can allow you to traverse these otherwise off-limits areas without having to resort to skulking about. Later in your main adventure through the Vatican, you'll be able to find a Blackshirt Disguise and this will allow you to walk through their barracks and military checkpoints without being harassed.

This can make certain side quests and mysteries much easier to complete, and even unlock new areas that you couldn't access otherwise. However, certain enemies like Captains can still see through your disguise, but at least you won't have to crouch down everywhere you go.

HOW TO USE COLLECTIBLE MAPS

When you first buy your Camera from Ernesto, you'll see that he sells a few brochures that act as maps for certain types of collectibles.You can buy or otherwise find maps like these from completing certain quests or mysteries, and they'll be added to your Adventure Book tally. However, you might find that they don't automatically appear on your map the next time you open your journal.

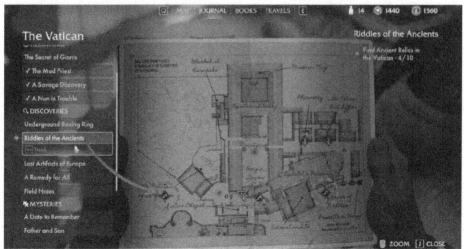

These brochures work in a very specific way - when viewing the map of your current area, you will need to select a Discovery Quest related to the collectible in question.

For example, if you have a map of Ancient Relics, you'll need to select the Discovery "Riddles of the Ancients" to see the icons appear on your map.

However, this will only apply to the area you are currently in, so if you want to see if there are any relics in an underground area, you will need to travel underground so that your default map in your journal displays that location, and then select the Discovery quest.

NOTE CATEGORIES CAN CHANGE

For those who love to collect every last item, it's worth understanding how Notes work in Indiana Jones and the Great Circle.

Notes are tallied in one of four categories: Adventure Notes (relating to the main quest), Fieldwork Notes (relating to specific sidequests), Mystery Notes (relating to short Mystery puzzles), and Field Notes (which encompass all unrelated notes for a given area).

Your Journal will track the number of Notes for a given category, but not everything you see listed under that category actually counts. Maps, for example — both the ones you find and the ones Indy sketches himself — do not count toward a Note total.

Some Notes will also initially be listed in the Field Notes section, despite not actually counting as a Field Note, and will move to a relevant Fieldwork category once that side quest has been unlocked. An example of this are the Inscriptions you need to take photos of for Antonio. They will be first listed as Field Notes, but after you are asked to photograph all ten of them, they will then be located in the Fieldwork Notes section for his side quest.

WEARING YOUR CLASSIC OUTFIT HELPS IN COMBAT

If you know you're going to be fighting, you should switch to Indy's traditional outfit where possible.

Doing this will grant you Fortitude, which allows you to take more hits in combat by adding a gold bar to your health. You can't switch outfits while in combat, but if you're in a crypt and you know there's zero reason to look like a man of the cloth, might as well toss on the fedora. While certain areas may force you to wear a disguise, places far from civilian area like tombs don't have that requirement.

That Gold bar of Fortitude is also what governs your ability to use Indy's Lucky Hat Skill, which gives you a second wind if you get knocked out by grabbing it off the ground. It takes time to recharge, so don't get too reckless after getting a second chance at life!

WALKTHROUGH

PROLOGUE - SOUTH AMERICA

The Golden Idol

❖ *Enter the Blood Temple*

When the game begins, you'll be treated to a recreation of Raiders of the Lost Ark's iconic opening. There's more than a few fun homages and shot for shot remakes, and you can start by either following your three Peruvian guides, or just racing off on your own down the clear path through the jungle.

Once you start going down an incline, head to the right to a thick jungle underbrush, and interact with it to move it aside with the help of your guides. One of the porters comes face to face with a creepy carving, and flees.

Keep moving past the carving until you come to a stream, and head left to travel upstream.

The path will continue across the stream once you reach a clearing, but you can keep heading up the left side to find a fun secret: the remains of Forrestall's campsite. There's a book that's been left behind in the camp that you can take: Warriors of the Clouds (it's entirely optional).

Crossing the stream, look for a pathway heading upward, and follow it to find a tree with a trail of white flowers, and a dart embedded at its base you can inspect.

After the scene, keep heading along the trail, and press the jump button by a low ledge to vault up and continue up the slope. When you reach a fallen branch along the path, interact with it to raise it up so you can continue.

In the next scene straight from the movie, Satipo will hand you the final piece of the map, and your other guide, Barranca, will try and make his move. Press the indicated prompt to perform a whip crack, and the startled man will flee, leaving you with just one guide left.

Note that you can also press your Journal button (J on PC) to pull out the famous map and inspect it yourself. This will also briefly highlight where to go in case you need to get your bearings.

The Chachapoyan temple's entrance is quite close now, as you need only climb the hill by the water where you'll find a series of stone steps leading to a dark and foreboding cave.

❖ Find the Golden Idol

With Satipo close behind, head into the cave and along the path to brush away a giant section of webbing (if you're not a fan of spiders, you may want to brace yourself, as you'll need to clear Satipo's back).

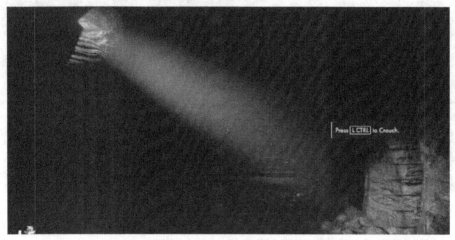

Just up ahead, you'll run into your first trap, which rival archaeologist Forrestall was unfortunately unaware of. There's another trap just beyond, so be sure to crouch down and hug the left wall to avoid the light as you move forward.

In the next room, you'll need to use your whip to swing across the gap. Look up at the fallen log and crack your whip (F on PC) to latch onto it, and then move off the ledge to swing to the other side.

Finally, you'll be in the hall of the Golden Idol, and while Satipo thinks there's nothing to fear, he's a little mistaken.

After pressing a torch into a hexagonal tile on the floor, you'll be met with a dart, and here is where things will differ from the movie just a bit. You won't be able to recreate Indy's nimble dance between the tiles, so instead you'll need to trigger certain safety tiles that disarm the row ahead.

To find the right ones, look for a hexagonal tile with a circle in the middle, and press down on it with your torch. Wait for the row of tiles ahead to recede, and then slowly crouch up to find the next tile with the circle in the middle.

You'll need to do this once more after heading up the stairs, so don't get too excited when you draw close to the Golden Idol.

Once you reach the prize, you'll be prompted to pull out a relevant item from your satchel (Tab on PC), and then interact with the idol. Recreate that iconic bit of adjusting the sand in the bag, and make the snatch and grab.

Quickly race back through the hall and through the hail of darts, and take a left to find that Satipo has already crossed back over the gap.

You'll need to toss the idol to him, so press the indicated prompt to ready your aim and then throw it to him. When he leaves without tossing you the whip, you'll need to run and jump across instead.

When the famous rolling ball appears, you'll need to sprint as well as move forward to outrun the death trap. A series of voices from the movie will begin to clue you in as to what's really going on, just before the scene ends with Indiana Jones waking up from a riveting dream back in Marshall College.

MARSHALL COLLEGE

The Break-In

❖ *Find the Intruder*

When Indy leaves his office to investigate the noise, you'll see a large trail of mud and debris leading down the hall.

Follow it to find a destroyed lounge room with a toppled bookcase below a hole in the window, and take the stairs up to the left.

Follow the light of a flickering lamp on the floor, and take a right at the top of the stairs to follow the very large footprints down another hall to overlook a museum exhibit below.

42

Take the path right back down some stairs until you reach a large circular desk. An open doorway can be found to the left, and next to it, a notice board with a paper you can pick up - a Campus Overview Map for Marshall College (useful if you get turned around).

Head through the first wing of the exhibit, and on the other side of the large doors you'll find the intruder - a giant of a man who doesn't look like he's here for sightseeing.

While this fight is something of an intro to combat, don't expect it to last long. Old Indy's a bit rusty with it being a year since his last adventure. You can try landing some punches with either trigger (or mouse button on PC), or even try blocking (V or Alt on PC). Once he grabs you, you'll have to mash your punching buttons to break free.

After a few quick bouts and grabs, Indy will slash the giant's face with the strange necklace, and then get knocked out. You'll get him next time.

The next morning, Dr. Jones' good friend Marcus Brody will wake you up with some smelling salts, and you'll begin to take stock of what the mystery man was after.

❖ *The Exhibit Puzzle*

Indiana Jones and the Great Circle has its fair share of puzzles, and will start you off with a fairly straightforward one: One of the display cases in this exhibit has been

43

smashed, with artifacts now strewn across the floor. There's something missing here, but you'll have to place the artifacts in the right spot to figure out what's been taken.

Luckily, there's no real penalty for placing any of the artifacts in the wrong spot, and Marcus or Indy himself will quickly realize when something isn't right. If you're playing with puzzles on a light difficulty, one of them will already be placed in the correct spot to give you a head start.

The Bastet Statue belongs with one of the stands with the Egyptian flag of the current era (green with a crescent moon and three stars), but since there are two such stands, look for the one on the left with a picture of the cat-headed god.

The Terracotta Relief belongs on the stand with the flag of Iraq (black, white, and green stripes with a red trapezoid on the left featuring two stars). Look for the images of similar looking reliefs next to where the Bastet Statue goes.

The Ivory Case is one of two artifacts from Syria, the flag with the three red stars in the middle, and features a series of Ugraritic letters on the side. Check on the far right side of the display for a picture showing the lettering to know where to place it.

The Funerary Mask is also from Syria, and its solid gold design best fits with the depictions of other priceless jewels in the middle of the display, left of a conspicuously absent Egyptian display case.

Once all five relics have been returned to their rightful displays, Indy will deduce the missing artifact is a Cat Mummy from a dig he attended in Siwa, Egypt.

❖ *Investigate the Theft*

Now that you know what's been taken, you'll need some more intel on the thief himself. Marcus will suggest you follow the trail of destruction, but first, let's make a small detour.

Head back through the exhibit back to the room with the round desk where you got the map for Marshall College. Look around on the desk, and you can spot a small card to pick up. This Faculty Card is one of many Notes you'll be able to collect during your adventure - some like this one are related to your current Adventure Quest, others for miscellaneous Fieldwork, and some that relate to Side Quests or Mysteries. Many will provide context and clues about the locations you visit, and finding them will earn you some Adventure Points, which you can think of as experience towards learning skills later in the game.

Head back to the ruined exhibit, and this time look for a trail of debris heading the opposite direction down a long hallway.

Look for an open door marked the Janitor's Closet, and inside you can find a Blackshirts Article on some shelving near the back.

You can also dip into the Nurse's Office on the right further down the hall. There's a cabinet against the wall you can open to find a Bandage. You don't actually need it now, but you can hold several at once so it's worth stocking up early.

Take a left before the end of the hall to head past where your office was, re-tracing your steps to where you may have noticed the giant fallen bookshelf in the lounge. The giant's necklace can be seen dangling from the broken window, but you'll need a way up.

Start lifting up the bookshelf until Marcus helps you push it all the way back up, and then climb up so you can grab the Giant's Pendant. Marcus will ask that you return back to your office, but there's a few more interesting things to find first.

Head up the stairs the same as you did the night before, but this time take a left through another small lounge on the second floor. Here you can find the Strange Aeons #1 Comic Book for your Notes.

Head through the nearby hallway, and look for a cart full of books. On it, you'll find a Baseball Card on one of the books.

Just down this hall, look on the left to find Dr. Jones' own classroom - Arch 2A - which you may remember from the movies. Inside you can find an apple on the desk (eating these will give you extra stamina reserve), and you can search your desk and some of the student desks for some notes.

Head down either staircase to return to Indy's office, and be sure to look behind his desk. Here you'll find a drawing of a Temple Map (The Forbidden Eye is a reference to the temple featured in the Indiana Jones ride at Disneyland!).

❖ *The Adventure Begins*

Once inside your office backroom, Indy and Marcus will deduce that the necklace came from the Vatican Secret Archive, and Indy will immediately begin packing his suitcase.

Inside, you'll find a present left from Marion, who was with Indy on his last adventure to find the Ark of the Covenant. Things didn't exactly work out between them, but the journal will prove to be incredibly useful.

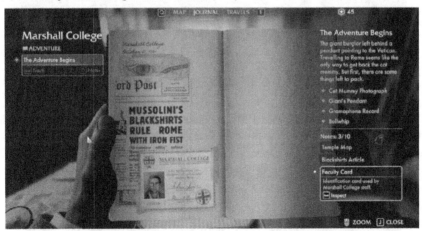

Your Journal will hold the sum of your knowledge as you start your adventure around the globe. All the notes, maps, and quests you find will all be catalogued here along with sketches and even some hand-drawn maps Indy will make himself to help guide you. You'll want to consult it frequently to figure out what to do next, or check on clues you may have found.

For now, you'll need to pack the essentials, which can all be found in your office (some will now become Notes tallied in your Journal):

48

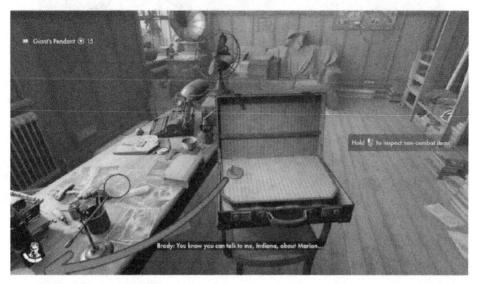

- The Cat Mummy Photograph is located on the far wall on a corkboard full of other photographs.

- The Giant's Pendant has been left on the book next to the suitcase, and can be placed in the suitcase itself.

- The Grampophone Record is located by the window next to the record player, and should also be placed in the suitcase.

- Indy's trusty Bullwhip is found on the shelves to the right of where the Cat Mummy photo was.

Once you have all the essentials packed, it will be time to set off on your big adventure. If you didn't collect all 10 Notes found around the college, don't worry - you'll be able to revisit this location whenever you like by accessing the Travels section of your Journal to tie up loose ends at a later date.

For now, your next destination lies in Italy. Indiana Jones is off to The Vatican City, to find The Stolen Cat Mummy.

THE VATICAN

The Stolen Cat Mummy - Castel Sant'Angelo

❖ *Enter Castel Sant'Angelo*

Your friend on the inside of the Vatican has promised to meet you at The Village Steps, which is located on the far side of a large circular castle. The bad news is it's crawling with members of Benito Mussolini's fascist militia known as "Blackshirts". The good news is you don't have to feel bad about beating these thugs up!

Your first encounter with a Blackshirt is just under a nearby streetlight, and unlike the giant you fought at Marshall College, he's much more punchable. Note the yellow bars at the bottom of the screen that indicate Indy's stamina. Performing actions will quickly lower your stamina, so you can't just wail on him forever. That said, he's not likely to survive more than a few square hits on most difficulties.

If you want to practice more refined brawling, space out your attacks by waiting for the thug to try punching, and block the attack before countering with the opposite fist and he'll go down quick.

After he's down for the count, you'll find the rest of the yard clear, so hop onto the low rooftop bathed in light, and then look up to spy a railing with white rags you can attach your whip to.

Move forward against the wall to automatically climb up, and then shimmy to the left. Climbing like this will also degrade your stamina fairly quickly, but you can always stop moving for a moment to recover stamina as needed and then keep moving.

❖ *Bastione San Luca*

The central raised Castel is surrounded by four "bastions", and you'll find yourself climbing onto the Bastione San Luca.

Here you'll find two more Blackshirts conversing in the middle of the rampart, presenting a few choices for how to proceed. You're certainly welcome to run up and start punching, but Indy only has so much health, and with backup never far away, there's always the chance you'll get swarmed and overwhelmed.

Another alternative is to sneak around potential trouble, and then decide if you want to bypass threats entirely, or take them out quietly. To help you with the former, you can find several bottles stashed around the crates in this area. Tossing one will cause the Blackshirts to investigate, letting you sneak away.

You can also start to find Improvised Weapons here. Everything from brooms to wrenches or spades can be picked up, and while they can give you a boost in hand-to-hand combat, their real charm lies in performing silent takedowns from behind.

Wait until one of the Blackshirts walks inside the nearby building, and sneak up behind the remaining thug with an improvised weapon. When Indy raises his arm, attack to perform a takedown that also (surprisingly) won't make any noise to alert his friend.

Note the small circles in the bottom right when holding an improvised weapon. This indicates the durability of the item, and most things you pick up usually have three dots, which will all be used up to perform a silent takedown. This means you'll need to regularly look for new improvised weapons as you continue.

From here, sneak inside the building and look for the other guard to take him out as well while he looks out a window, or ignore him completely as the door next to him is locked. If you don't take both guards out, be sure to hide the body by grabbing it and placing it behind objects so it's not spotted.

Back at the entrance to the building, look on top of a wooden crate to find a Pope Article to add to your Field Notes. Some Notes are relevant to your current Adventure, while others like this one are tallied in your Field Notes section that help give context to the world.

Since the alleyway outside also leads to a locked door, and another door to the left outside requires a Rampart Key, the only way to progress is to look for a stairway down in the building.

51

You'll be above a small chapel room, and to find a way down, head into the next balcony room and look for a gap in the railing. Turn around and slowly walk backward to fall off the platform and grab the white railing below, then press the crouch button to drop to the floor below.

The room is empty, but be sure to look to the right of the door to the chapel to find a local Map of Castel Sant'Angelo. You can also turn around to find a spot on the wall by a coat rack that holds the Rampart Key for the door back above (we'll use it later).

Head into the Chapel of the Condemned and look for a note on the right, Caruso's Letter, before heading to the other side of the room.

❖ Reach the Top of the Castello

Grab a candlestick before slowly opening the door leading outside. Two Blackshirts will converse briefly, before one starts to patrol down the road between the high castle and the bastions. Take out the lone guard when his friend leaves, and stash his body back in the chapel where nobody will come looking.

The patrolling guard will stop at a barbed wire checkpoint to converse with another Blackshirt, making it a risky endeavor to try to get past them. Instead, look up above to the left along some scaffolding for a bar you can grab onto with your whip and then climb upwards.

From here, look for a flagpole to grapple with your whip and swing across (luckily it won't alert the guards below), and then sneak along the raised pathway past the checkpoint guard below.

Carefully drop down at the far end while keeping an eye on the patrolling guard, though you'll find the door here requires a Guard House Key. Just beyond the locked door, you can find a few small alcoves further up that make a great spot to ambush and stash the patrolling guard's body.

Past these alcoves, there's a doorway leading into a small barracks. A Blackshirt inside may or may not be looking out the window, so if you aren't able to get behind him, quickly charge in and overpower him before he can call for help.

The small barracks is a treasure trove of loot and worth inspecting thoroughly:

Look for a small red book labeled Punch Out 1 on top of a wooden footlocker below some filing cabinets. This is an Adventure Book, one of my collectible books you can find that can unlock skills for Indy. Each one costs a different amount of Adventure Points to learn, which is why finding Notes are so important!

Speaking of Notes, look on the table by the bunk beds to find Valeria's Letter, which is actually an important clue for something you'll be dealing with later in The Vatican.

Over on the wall, you can find the Guard House Key to unlock that door you passed by previously. You can also find a pouch of money (Italian Lira) that should clue you in that there will be things you'll need to buy on your adventure. Just remember what Indiana Jones says: "Fascists shouldn't be trusted with money." So help yourself!

Your target to breach the castle above will lead you further left out the door, but a couple of patrolling guards can make things tricky. Instead, head back right to return to the locked door where you'll be prompted to pull out the Guard House Key and head inside.

Upstairs you'll find a guard desk with a note on it, De Vito's Letter. Be sure to also check for a drawer nearby that holds both some Lira and Revolver Ammo!

Yes, Indiana Jones does have his trusty Revolver when you just can't be bothered for fisticuffs, but we highly recommend using a gun incredibly sparingly. Not only is ammo incredibly sparse and hard to come by, but using your gun is very, very loud, and will send everyone nearby running to join the fight. Because of this, it's best saved when you're either greatly outnumbered, or facing down other gun-toting thugs, and luckily none of the Blackshirts in the Vatican will be using guns.

There's some more Lira at the back desk by a typewriter, along with a Biscotti. Food items don't exactly restore health (you need Bandages for those) but eating one can give you extra temporary health or stamina depending on the food type, so chow down early and often!

Head upstairs to find a door leading out to the alley leading to your next destination, but there's a second patrolling guard around here. Luckily there's a way to bypass this guy too — just climb the ladder to the top floor of the guard house. Here you'll find another door to unlock with your key.

You can also hop through the opposite window to find a pathway leading all the way back to the Bastione San Luca where you arrived. Using the Rampart Key found in the chapel, you'll now have a shortcut back to the start of the castel.

Head out onto the top floor walkway, and you'll find a pathway leading to part of a building below the central castel, with some scaffolding. Wait for the two Blackshirts below to start wandering down, and sneak over to the scaffolding.

Attach your whip to the pole above, but since there's no wall to walk up, you'll instead need to hold the prompt (right click on PC) to dangle in place, allowing you to press up to climb upwards to the top of the scaffolding.

Continue climbing to the top of the building, and be sure to take in the view before looking for a small window to jump up and climb through into the main castel area.

❖ *Get to the Passetto di Borgo*

Now in the upper castle, head through the passage and look for some money by some playing cards on a barrel before heading upstairs.

Slowly approach the window and peek outside into a central courtyard where a guard is chatting with another, flanked by an attack dog. This can be bad news if you get spotted, as the dogs have a tendency to latch onto you, but if you do get attacked, try using your whip crack to scare them off.

Head around the passage to find a diverging path, and you'll soon find that you have several options for how to proceed:

Pathway 1 - The Rooftop Rampart

Possibly the most straightforward, though a bit reckless. As soon as the guard and his dog turn around, sneak out into the courtyard and look for stone stairs leading up above to the second floor, where one Blackshirt watches over a balcony.

You can knock him out and find that the ledge here has a series of poles you can swing between with your whip all the way to the side, but an easier path is up to the wooden stairs to the very top of the castle (there's also a passage below the stairs leading to a red military rations crate with money).

The narrow rampart here leads around the roof of the building where a lone Blackshirt patrols. With no cover, he's harder to sneak up on, but if you defeat him, you can drop down the other side where you'll find a zipline leading out of the castel and can ignore most of this area.

Pathway 2 - The Captain's Key

If you want to get the most out of this area, stick to the shadows and take the path through a small wine cellar on the left and into a garage area. A single Blackshirt wanders this area and can be taken out quietly when the guard and his dog aren't looking. Be sure to look in the center of the garage for a Tales of Dread #1 Comic Book Note on a radio table, and a red military rations crate nearby with money inside.

57

The room beyond has stairs leading up to the second floor, but be wary of a Blackshirt manning the spotlight above. You can spot a large gate on the far side of the courtyard, but it's locked and requires the Captain's Key. Be sure to also grab Mario's Note posted by the gate before retreating back to the stairs.

Quietly take out the man posted on the spotlight, and check the supply room nearby for another red military rations chest with Money and Revolver Ammo inside. Next door is the barracks, which has more supplies, money, and a Gizeh Postcard on the bottom bunk by the door.

Armed with an Improvised Weapon, slowly sneak into the Captains' Room. If you're

58

careful you can find him turned around, but if he spots you, rush him and beat him down with whatever you can find before he makes too much noise.

Look for the Captain's Key hanging on the wall to the left of the window, and be sure to also check by the door for Lucky Hat 1 - an Adventure Book that gives you a second chance if you get knocked out.

Note the small lockbox on the captain's desk. It may not look like it, but you can actually bust the thing open. You'll either need to use an improvised weapon or your revolver (but we don't recommend using a gun for the noise it makes). Inside, you can find a ton more Lira to swipe!

With the Captain's Key, you can head back down to the courtyard and slip around the guard and his dog to unlock the gate, and take the stairs up to the zipline.

❖ *Pathway 3 - The Bulls of Blood*

The last path is a little more tricky and involved, as it requires you to solve your first Mystery. You can locate this mystery by ducking into the stone building on the opposite side of the courtyard, which consists of three rooms, two dozing Blackshirts and one patrolling between them. Three notes here will all trigger the Mystery, which involves solving a puzzle to unlock a secret passage to a fourth note, and a way to bypass the locked gate.

For a full detailed walkthrough, check our Bulls of Blood Mystery Guide.

Whichever path you take, all roads will lead to a large zipline leading down to another bastione where the path to the Vatican can be found.

⋄ *Bastione San Marco*

Once you touch down on the bastion, you'll find the area clear of thugs. As an added bonus, you can look for a walkway that leads all the way back to the first bastione to unlock both the alley gate, and another door in the first building you entered that has one of the red military rations crate with a Money and Revolver Bullets. You'll now have an easy shortcut to move around the castel much faster, in case you need to return here later to pick up missed collectibles.

To proceed, look for a circular staircase descending into the bastione. A Blackshirt will start walking up, and you'll be prompted to disarm him using a Whip Crack. You can even grab the weapon he drops and club him with it!

Further up is a second thug, and this one you can practice holding the Whip button to drag him into your waiting arms, letting you perform a grab and unleash several strikes he won't be able to block.

Be ready to deal with one last Blackshirt near the end of the hall, and look for a small red chest with an Adventure Book on top, Brawler 1.

Be sure to look around for Bandages if you need them, then head outside to find the passage leading to The Village Steps.

One last fascist is blocking the path, and this one is known as a Bruiser. These guys are bigger than the other thugs (though not as big as that giant), and will hit harder, and can even stagger you through your blocking.

The good news is there's a few Improvised Weapons lying around. Pick up the biggest one and hold down the attack button as you move toward him. Let go as you meet to launch a heavy attack that should knock him back, and then follow up with a few quick hits to put him down before he can react.

With all the thugs out of the way, head along the rest of the path to be met by a friendly face, Father Antonio.

After a brief scene, he'll unlock a door for you, and you can unlock the gate at the far end to finish your time at the Castel, and enter the Vatican City to resume your search for The Stolen Cat Mummy.

The Stolen Cat Mummy - Vatican City

Following the Break-In at Marshall College, Indy has successfully infiltrated Vatican City by way of the Castel Sant'Angelo. Thanks to his friend on the inside, Father Antonio, Indy can start looking for clues in earnest while trying to keep a low profile.

Below, you'll find a complete Walkthrough for beginning to explore the Vatican City, including finding the secrets of the library, getting yourself a camera, and finding mysterious inscriptions all over the city, along with the locations of collectibles found in this area.

When Indy awakens the next morning, you'll find yourself in Antonio's Office in the Vatican Library. You'll also get a Note on Antonio in the form of a sketch in your journal.

After relaxing for a bit (be sure to grab a Cornetto and chow down for an achievement!), Antonio will ask for proof about the Cat Mummy Thief. Hand over the Giant's Pendant, and Antonio will mention the writings of a "mad" Father Crecenzo who mentioned giants that might fit the description. He'll also remember seeing the symbol from the pendant in the libraries' conservation room.

Once Antonio returns from his closet with a new pair of clothes, take the Clerical Suit from him to don your first (of several) disguises!

With this outfit (that you can swap between by taking out your satchel) you'll be able to blend in among the other priests of the Vatican... to an extent. It also comes with a small staff as part of the uniform, meaning you'll have a spare weapon on hand for emergencies, which can be fixed with a Repair Kit.

Not a moment too soon, as Father Ventura slips in to make his presence known. With the Pope indisposed due to illness, Ventura seemingly has the run of the place, and is responsible for opening the gates to Mussolini's Blackshirt fascists who have now set up checkpoints and camps all over the place. This won't be the last you see of this snake, so be on your guard whenever he's about.

❖ Search for the Symbol

Your search for the strange Vatican symbol begins in the Apostolic Library. With your Clerical Suit, you'll be able to wander the area without arousing any suspicion, so head along the upper floor to take the stairs down to the lower level.

There's not much you can do here, and you aren't allowed to leave the library yet, but you can find a small Briscola Flyer note on one of the tables by the windows.

Look for where a man is trying to replace some lightbulbs and head through the door marked "Conservatore Deila".

The room is quite sparse, but the wall behind the desk bears a cross,and below it the symbol that matches the Giant's Pendant. Interact with it and pull it to the side to reveal a hidden passageway!

Father Antonio will suddenly appear beside you, ready to help you explore. It looks pretty dark down there, so be sure to grab a candle from the table before heading inside.

❖ Explore the Secret Passage

Note that as you pass several braziers, you can hold your candle near them to automatically light them up, and give yourself more light to work with.

Keep heading down the passage, holding the candle high to light the way. At the bottom of the passageway, the room will open up to reveal several fallen shelves, and a sealed gate on your right.

Since you need to find another way to open the gate, toss the candle to the ground and duck under the fallen shelves to find a pool of water. Hop in and swim through a gap to come up on the other side of the gates.

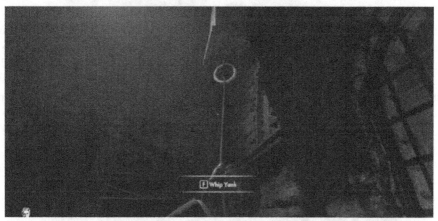

Head back over to where Antonio is waiting and use a Whip Crack on the rung above the gate, and yank it to unlock the gate, and grab your candle again before taking stock of the room.

In the far corner, you'll find the remains of the mad Father Crescenzo, who seems to have mysteriously died in his alchemical laboratory among his notes. Pick up and read his Mad Scribbles, and Antonio will also point out a crude map that Father Crescenzo has also drawn. It's difficult to make out, but the X marks seem to correlate to inscriptions that Antonio noticed in certain places around The Vatican.

Intent to find out more about these inscriptions, Antonio will suggest you photograph them and bring the photos back to his office. While he doesn't have a camera, the janitor Ernesto at the Vatican Post Office might have one for sale. Antonio will then give you a special key, one that opens any Clerical Door marked with a stained glass cross (just be sure you're wearing your disguise when entering such locations).

Before you leave, be sure to search the lab thoroughly. Over by the gate you opened up, you can find a mysterious Ancient Relic that seems very out of place. This will begin a Discovery Quest to track down a total of 10 such Ancient Relics hidden around The Vatican.

❖ *Get to the Post Office*

Secret Character Interactions

66

As you exit the secret underground chamber, you may hear a nun struggling with something in the library by the stairs. The Game Manual refers to these as Secret Interactions - they aren't big enough to be considered side quests, but they are tasks you can help assist with. Whenever you hear any random character complaining about something - usually a missing item or request, you can find the item the character needs (usually nearby). Try grabbing the highlighted book and then place it on a nearby table, and you'll be awarded some Adventure Points, which you can never have too many of!

With the Clerical Key, you are now free to leave the Apostolic Library. Go ahead and unlock both Clerical Doors on both floors, and then head down the connecting staircase.

Before you leave, be sure to look next to the exit door for an incredibly handy map of Vatican City, which is where you'll be spending a lot of time in for the foreseeable future.

Stepping out into Belvedere Courtyard, you'll find Indy's world has vastly opened up. There is a deceptively large amount of places to explore in Vatican City, with collectibles and secrets hiding around every corner. You're free to beeline through the main Adventure (and you should, at least until getting the Camera), but feel free to explore... so long as you don't anger the fascists.

Your Clerical Suit works well enough to not be attacked on sight by the Blackshirts, but there are some rules you'll need to be mindful of:

- When there is an eye icon next to Indy's portrait, it means the Blackshirts are watching you. If you behave rashly, use your whip, or steal money from them in plain sight, they will attack. Unlike the Castel, there are a lot more fascists here that can quickly overwhelm you, so it's best to either run and hide in a building or rooftop, or just avoid negative attention altogether.

- Certain areas of Vatican City are off-limits even to the priests, and these military checkpoints are marked in red on your map. You'll need good reason to go sneaking in these areas, as getting caught in an area densely populated by enemies won't end well.

Still, there are a few tents on the side of the courtyard that aren't technically off-limits, but you will have to make sure nobody is watching when you swipe their money - and you'll need a fair amount to buy that camera.

Check out the first tent on the left to carefully swipe some Lira, and check out the Theft Report Note, as it will start a Fieldwork Sidequest in your journal for A Savage Discovery!

In the adjoining tent, swipe some more Lira, and look for a red military rations crate that doubles as a locked safe, but where's the combination?

68

Check the desk drawers nearby, and you'll find a Ticket Stub with a hole conveniently punched next to two numbers, and an arrow pointing to the back. Rotate the stub to see the other two numbers, which will give you the combination: 5238. Unlock the safe (carefully) to gain a lot of Lira (which you'll need to buy that camera) and the Splinter Smash Adventure Book!

By the next set of tents, you can find a signpost depicting points of interest. This will serve as your Fast Travel Points, and you'll be able to return to this signpost by finding others at the listed names, which can be useful for skirting Blackshirt patrols.

Before leaving the courtyard, you should also check the tent on the opposite side of the fountain with a jeep parked in the back. Inside you'll find more Lira to swipe, and an Adventure Book for Pep 1.

Head left down to Via Di Belvedere, where you'll find the large door ahead sealed by fascists who aren't letting anyone in. Unfortunately, this is exactly where you need to go to reach the Post Office, so you'll need to do a bit of inventive parkour. There are more than a few ways to reach it, but one of them in particular has something worth finding along the way.

From the sealed door, look to the left for a small alleyway with a seemingly dead end. Luckily, there's some scaffolding work on the right side, and you can launch your whip at the bar above while out of view of the Blackshirts.

Climb up the scaffolding to find a man having his morning coffee, seemingly undisturbed by your acrobatics. Just beyond him, look for a barrel in the far corner that holds an Adventure Book called Climbing Ace 1 for you to claim.

Jump up onto the roof past the barrel with the book, and take a good look at the back street below. You're now in a restricted zone, so your Clerical Suit won't be doing you any favors.

Luckily, there happens to be a zipline next to you, and you can ride it all the way to the low roof outcropping on the left side of the backstreet, putting you right across from the Post Office.

Look for an open window next to some scaffolding across from where you land off the zipline, and wait until the guard and his dog move away before making a run for the building. Once inside, you won't be bothered.

While you're in this hallway, you can find a really nice Risotto ai Funghi Recipe for your notes, and then use the Clerical Key you got on the door with the cross to enter the Post Office.

Two priests will be blocking the far door trying to see what the Blackshirts are up to, leaving you to enter the janitor's room (Facchino) to speak to Ernesto. While initially unwilling, he'll eventually settle for letting it go for the price of 379 Lira.

If you've been diligent in relieving the fascists of their money, you may already have twice that amount. If not, you'll need to go hunting for spare change in the tents and checkpoints around the city.

It's also possible to revisit Castel Sant'Angelo now that the area outside the Post Office is no longer restricted. Just head south and head up the stairs to the large wall battlements and follow them east to revisit the area where Antonio led you through.

Once you have the goods, accept his price, and the camera will be yours! This useful tool can be used to snap pictures of important objects and locales, and will double as Notes for your Journal. Any time you see a camera icon appear in the corner of the screen, you'll know there's something to take a picture of.

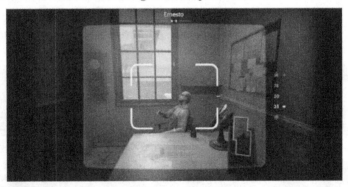

When pulling out your Camera, look for a square reticle, and move close, zoom in or out, and position yourself until the lines become clear before snapping the photo. Like Notes, they'll give Adventure Points for a successful shot, and some photos can even be given to people.

Try taking a photo of Ernesto to score an easy Achievement, plus a Note for your Journal!

You may also notice that Ernesto has two other things for sale. These brochures act like Treasure Maps: Buying one will unlock a new Discovery in your Journal, allowing you to track the locations of Mysteries or Adventure Books in the city:

Ernesto's Lost and Found	
Item Name	**Cost**
Vatican Mysteries	300L
Vatican Books	300L

❖ *Photograph the Inscriptions*

With a camera in hand, you're now free to take photos of many things, but most important are some of the inscriptions mentioned by Antonio that Father Crescenzo himself has marked on a map.

As you leave the Janitor's room in the Post Office, a few things have actually changed The door is now clear to unlock with your Clerical Key, as the military have pulled out (though they still patrol the area). You can also find a crumpled note on a desk nearby, and reading Catherine's Letter will trigger a new Fieldwork Sidequest to learn more about Father Crescenzo in The Mad Priest.

Before you go off inscription hunting, there's a few other things of note to inspect. Leave the Post Office through the front door and head down the road past the checkpoint, where you can snap a photo of some Cobblestone Workers.

73

Just to the right of the workers where the road curves, look for a notice board, and you'll find a Mystery Note concerning a Missing Cat Flyer, starting the A Free Spirit Mystery to track down the prestigious Signor Smushki, who should be located not far from here.

Head back up the road toward Belvedere Courtyard, and look for a building next to the Post Office that is home to a pharmacy. Sister Valeria is running things as best she can, but the Blackshirts have appropriated all of her medicine. If you happen to stumble across said medicine, you'll be handsomely rewarded for stealing it back.

This will start the Discovery Quest A Remedy for All to locate 15 such vials, which can be exchanged for various Adventure Books:

Sister Valeria's Pharmacy	
Item Name	Total Medicine Required
Moxie 1	5 Medicine Each
Shaping Up 1	
Moxie 2	10 Medicine Each
Shaping Up 2	

Moxie 3	15 Medicine Each
Shaping Up 3	

Be sure to snap a photo of Sister Valeria before you go, and if you want to get a head start on those medicine vials, one is fairly close by.

Head back down to the backstreet behind the Vatican Post Office, and you'll be able to walk past the patrolling guard and his dog without worry. Right at the end of the street, above an entrance to a cellar, you can find a bench with a medicine vial sitting in plain view.

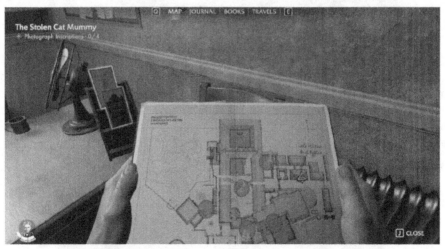

Though multiple inscription locations have been marked on your map, you only need four to bring back to Antonio. That said, you can eventually collect photos of all 10, so it really doesn't matter which ones you photograph, especially if you're keen to do a bit of exploring and side questing. This particular guide will focus on four inscriptions that are fairly easy to find and not hiding in restricted zones, marked on the map image above.

Head back up Via Di Belvedere back towards the courtyard, into the area where the door used to be sealed, and look for a metal gate to the side leading into a garden area.

Head past all the workers and scaffolding to the far corner of the garden, and look for a small stone fountain against the wall with a strange looking inscription of two figures and a larger gold one holding a sword. Snap it with your camera to capture the first inscription.

(These notes will eventually be added to a Fieldwork Sidequest, but they may appear as Field Notes at first)

❖   *Secret Character Interaction*

While taking a photo of the inscription, you might spot a paintbrush lying on the side of the fountain. There's likely a female worker in the middle of the gardens worried about her missing brush. You can bring it over and place it next to her to earn some extra Adventure Points!

    ◈   *Second Inscription*

Head all the way back to Belvedere Courtyard for an easy inscription location.

You'll find it along the central fountain in the courtyard, on the side facing the Apostolic Library. Look for the figure holding a broken sword, and snap a photo of it.

    ◈   *Third Inscription*

From the courtyard, head to the far end where a massive propaganda stage has been erected (and steer clear of the captain with the black and yellow cap inspecting his troops, as he will spot you as the fake you are!). Be sure to snap a photo of the Stage Construction to add it to your notes.

Move around behind the stage to find a lot of scaffolding away from prying eyes, and start climbing until you reach a high balcony above the courtyard.

You'll be alongside the Tower of Borgia now, and the high balcony is home to a single Blackshirt who shouldn't mind your presence as long as you aren't slinging your whip around. Follow the balcony away from the guard to the far end to find another fountain with an inscription depicting several fallen figures.

While you're here, you may want to climb up the scaffolding where the guard is posted to reach the highest balcony, where you'll find a window into a section of the Apostolic Palace, where you can find a Note to trigger the House of God Mystery.

⋄ *Fourth Inscription*

From the hallway with the House of God Mystery, hop out the opposite window where you'll be high above the Borgia Courtyard.

Carefully move along the ledge to climb up to a higher roof on the right, and you'll find a fountain to photograph depicting several graves. This should be the last one you'll need to take a photo of (for now).

Head back to the Apostolic Library (or take your time to scout out some Fieldwork Sidequests if you want). Don't worry about the other inscriptions just yet, as you'll likely run into them doing sidequests or later in the main adventure anyway.

Secret Character Interaction

As you enter the stairway into the library, you may overhear a group of nuns lamenting having to go back to their convent without something to remember Father Antonio by. You can help them out by taking out your camera to snap a photo of him and then give a copy to the nuns by placing it on the table next to them!

While you're heading back to Antonio, be sure to look for some more photo ops, including a priest Adjusting a Painting on the stairwell, some Fixture Work at the top of the stairs, and a Nun Study Group on the lower floor of the library.

Once you're back in Antonio's office, take the photos out from your satchel and place them on the desk. Using the magnifying glass, inspect each photo in turn until you find the prompt over a specific part of the photo.

79

Finally, Antonio will ask you to translate a passage of Latin, which points to the Tower of Nicholas the Fifth as the entrance to an "underworld" where the tomb of a giant is.

When he mentions needing the blood of the five sacred wounds, he'll place one of the photos back down, prompting you to inspect one last time with the magnifying glass to find that you'll need the blood of Christ - aka a bottle of sanctified wine!

The next part of your journey in The Vatican lies deep beneath the Tower of Nicholas V, but feel free to explore around as you head back that way.

The Stolen Cat Mummy - The Tower of Nicholas V (Underworld)

After exploring the Vatican City for clues to the identity of the Stolen Cat Mummy thief, strange inscriptions found around the city have pointed to a secret Underworld below the Tower of Nicholas V. Below, you'll find a complete Walkthrough for navigating the hidden chambers and tunnels of the Underworld, how to solve the Sacred Wounds Puzzle, and uncovering the Giants Tomb, along with the locations of collectibles found in this area.

Once Indy and Antonio have deduced the location of the Giant's Tomb, you'll be tasked with finding a path into the "Underworld" below the Tower of Nicholas V, which is located at the end of Via Di Belvedere. There's plenty to explore along the way, and you can take the time to uncover some Fieldwork Sidequests and Mysteries if you like.

Upon reaching the Tower of Pope Nicholas V, be sure to duck around a patrolling Captain as you enter.

On the far side of the tower's interior, you can find a creepy altar full of stone statues and a Strange Mural you can take a picture of with your camera.

With the wine given to you by Father Antonio, splash some of it in the receptacle and the mural of the demon and angel will jut outward, allowing you to rotate it.

To solve this puzzle, rotate the mural so that the demon is falling downward with the angel above, and it will unlock a path into the Underworld.

❖ *Underworld Walkthrough*

As you begin to descend into the depths, look for a pot of sticks by the entrance and grab one. You can hold it by one of the candles at the altar to light up a torch, and then use it to light more braziers as you go deeper.

Navigating the twisting catacombs, you can find wall sconces with unlit torches you can light up. Aside from helping light the path, it's also a good way to see where you've already been.

At the end of the tunnel, a larger chamber will open up beyond a gate, introducing your next big puzzle.

◆ *The Sacred Wounds Puzzle*

In the middle of the chamber is a large mural of Jesus Christ on the cross. Be sure to take a photo of the Sacred Wounds Mural. Note that you can continue to take photos of puzzle elements to get some hints from Indy himself.

This puzzle involves a painting of Jesus on the cross, basins or cups for wine that reveal Roman numerals I, II, III, IV, (these represent numbers 1, 2, 3, and 4) and little levers near Jesus's image at the center of the room with the same numbers that you can adjust by approaching them. Several paintings and torches you can light with their own wine pouring areas area located around the chamber and off to the side.

To start this puzzle, pour some more wine in the receptacle in front of the mural, and five levers will appear near all of the sacred wounds on Jesus: two on his hands, two on his feet, and one on his chest. Each lever has a series of roman numerals next to them, and your job is to figure out which number each lever should be at.

Start by looking to the right of the Sacred Wounds Mural to find a Walking on Water mural to take a photo of.

The keys to this puzzle lies in applying more wine to the different receptacles. Do so here and the wine will react by forming a number: 3. The other half of this key is correlating the mural to the Sacred Wounds mural. Note that there is a distinct gold circle around Jesus' right foot (your left).

With this in mind, head back to the main mural and go to the lever by his right foot (the lower left side of the mural) and push it to III or 3.

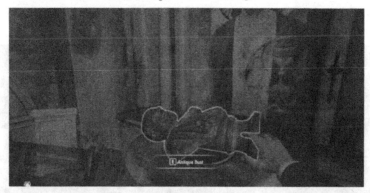

Next, move to the left to find a Holy Chalice mural to take a photo of. Note that it also has a receptacle, but a statue bust is blocking it, so toss it aside.

Pour the wine in the unblocked receptacle to reveal the number 2, and note the circle around his left hand. Move the corresponding lever at the main mural.

Looking further left, there's a doorway you can head through, only for it to seal shut behind you. Oops. While you're here, take a photo of the Body of Christ mural before pouring wine to see the number 2. Note the circle around his right hand.

To escape this little trap, look for a side passage leading to another room with the Spear of Longinus statue you can snap a photo of, and place wine in the receptacle to reveal the number 3. The spear tip itself has a circle around it, which should clue you in to where the spear stabbed Jesus.

Grab a large Improvised Weapon off the ground, and smash the wall where you can see the bricks to create an opening back in the main room.

Finally, there's one more mural behind a sealed gate to the right of the central mural but luckily there's a tiny crawlspace to shimmy through. Pull on the chain on the other side to open the gate, and then snap a photo of the Anointment of Jesus mural and the circle around his left foot, and then pour one last bit of wine to find the number 4.

Return to the Sacred Wounds mural and pull the levers so that each section matches the wine numbers you saw:

- Right Hand: 2 (II)
- Left Hand: 2 (II)
- Right Foot: 3 (III)

- Left Foot: 4 (IV)
- Body: 3 (III)

If done correctly, the levers will recede, and the mural will slide away to reveal a deeper tomb beyond.

❖ *Find the Warrior Giant's Tomb*

Now you'll be in a much older necropolis full of burial chambers along the walls.

When the path splits, you'll find that heading straight leads to a dead end, with a pedestal that seems to be missing something.

Recall the obstruction of a statue bust at one of the Sacred Wound Murals, and return to grab it, and then carry it over to place the bust on the pedestal. The weight will open the gate, allowing you to grab a secret note, the Trapped Account.

Back at the intersection, take the path to the left that goes straight to an open area with a pillar leading down to a lower level, and a skeleton by the low wall that holds a Burial Chamber Key.

To the right is a sealed gate, but there is a way to get to the other side. Head back down the long hall and look for a small room on the left.

Look upwards, and you should find a small hole near the ceiling to crawl through leading to the other side of that locked gate.

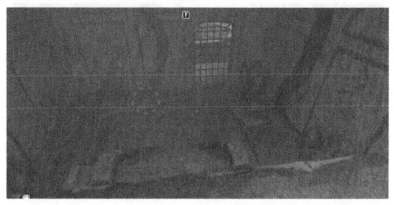

Use your Whip to yank the iron rung that opens the gate, and then look on the ground for an Explorer's Journal to add to your Notes.

As you exit the room, look for a small passageway to the right leading down to the bottom of that large pillar, and scan the walls for a Jerusalem Cross to snap a photo of.

Back on the upper level, there's a creepy room with statues surrounding a tomb on the right, and a main path going left from the pillar.

We're in the progress of solving this secret, check back soon!

Just to the left of that is another small room that connects to a flammable slab of wood back up on the narrow path.

Either way leads to a second note, some Paranoid Writing.

Taking the main path leads to a large gap you'll need to swing across, but Indy can't hold his torch while swinging. Toss the torch over to the other side of the gap first, then swing over to and pick it up.

As you do, you may notice a wall of wood you can burn away to reveal a small chamber that has a Tomb Fresco you can snap a photo of along the corner wall.

Finally, the path will end past a group of skeletons in a gate you can use the Burial Chamber Key to unlock. Before you lies a grand necropolis where the Tomb of the Warrior Giant lies.

Be sure to snap a photo of the Tomb of the Warrior Giant as you approach, which reads "Tomb of Augur the Giant, who died in the service of God at Ascalon." Spooky stuff.

When trying to interact with the tomb to open it, Indy will initially have no luck, so you'll need to find another way.

Look for two small stairs on either side of the tomb that have a stone shield emblem on them, but the one on the left is missing, with a hole you can reach through. Interact with the hole to trigger a mechanism.

Check the other stairs to find the stone shield has rotated, and can now be removed. Take it off and interact with the hole to unlock the tomb. Maybe not the way you intended.

Indy will search the remains of the giant to find a Warrior Giant's Parchment, which indicates the "Fountain of Confession" as an entrance to a sanctum for the Nephilim. Unfortunately, even more cave-ins send a tractor from the Excavation Yard above crashing down, and Indy will be flung into a side passage as the rubble blocks you from returning to the tomb.

❖ *Find a Way Out*

You'll need to find a way back to the tomb if you want to climb through the hole that tractor made, but it won't be a straightforward path.

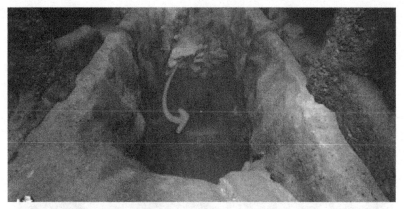

Head down the stairs past a creepy statue to a pit leading down to water. You can swing across but there's nothing on the other side, however if you lower yourself down on the whip, there's a ledge above the water you can swing to.

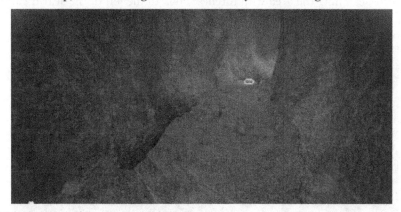

On this small ledge connecting the pools of water, you can find a short tunnel that has an Ancient Relic.

Drop into the water and swim forward, ducking down to swim through the flooded passages.

Once you reach a larger open flooded area, there's a bit of dry ground you can swim to, and across from the ledge is a sculpture of Oceanus you can snap a photo of.

Look in the corner of the flooded room for a small break in the wall you can swim through, leading to a new passageway you can shimmy through.

On the other side, your good fortune will soon turn sour with the arrival of Blackshirts searching the area with torches. Look to the left of the sealed gate for a passage, and check the ground for a two-handed Improvised Weapon.

If you move quickly, you can head up to find some alcoves to hide behind as the two fascists move forward to attempt to locate your position. Stick to the right side as they move along the other route and take them both from behind.

You may notice one of the Blackshirts is a Medic, and will drop Bandages, but can also revive allies you have knocked out.

Grab a torch from one of the thugs and keep moving forward to find a passage with a wooden plank down to a lower level.

Ditch the torch here and look for another Improvised Weapon before crouching through the hole, and you'll find yourself in a large part of the Necropolis that is overrun by Blackshirts.

It's important to remember you don't have to defeat all the enemies in this room - you gain nothing for defeating them unless you just really love beating up fascists. Still, you'll likely want to take out a few of them so they don't spot you as you try to make your way to the upper level.

To start, take out the closest Blackshirt with his back to you and stash him in the corner, then advance cautiously. While there are some guys on the high balcony, they won't be able to spot you in the shadows down below.

Two more fascists will patrol as a team through the lower floor, and since they are hard to split up, you may not want to engage them unless you can distract one of them by throwing a weapon. Instead, wait until they cross to the right side of the room to hug the left wall where a section of water is, and swim across to the other side.

A lone Blackshirt is guarding this place with his back turned to the water, so head up the stairs to the left to bypass him and reach the second floor.

At the top, another thug is guarding the broken bridge, but will wander back over to a gate near a brazier, making it a good time to whack him over the head.

After this, you can latch onto the chandelier to swing across the bridge, and take a quick right to avoid the last two thugs at the end of the intact bridge.

Move slowly into the next room where a Medic is wandering by a seated Bruiser. Let them talk for a bit, and then smack the Medic from behind. Next, lure the Brusier out from his seated position by tossing a torch elsewhere to take him out quietly next

You'll find all the gates here are sealed, but a fallen statue bust holds the clue. By placing it near one of the gates on a pedestal, it will open the gate. First, look for a pedestal in the corner on the lower part of the room, opening a gate to a small room with an Ancient Relic.

Place the bust on the pedestal to the left of the other gate to open up an exit, and leave this area behind.

Be sure to look for a slightly open passage on the left in the next room, leading to a mural of a Lover's Tomb you can take a photo of.

Look for another door to open that triggers some braziers to light up, and proceed on to find a series of wooden beams you can latch onto to climb upwards to a higher ledge.

Climbing up the second plank, you can swing over to find a new path.

Crawl through the next hole into a hallway with an empty pedestal next to a sealed gate, and search the next room to spot a bust already on a pedestal (don't touch the one already on a pedestal here or it will seal the door).

Instead, look in the corner of the room for a discarded bust behind some debris, and pick that one up instead.

Return the discarded bust to the pedestal in the hall to open the other gate, and you'll find another pedestal, along with a section of weak wall you can smash open with an Improvised Weapon.

Grab the bust in the next room to take off its pedestal, and place it on the one in the other room to open a gate to another Ancient Relic.

Return to the hallway to enter an area full of debris you need to duck under, leading to a flooded room on the right. As you cross to the far side, stay low to avoid being seen by a Blackshirt patrol on the other side of a gate.

While you can use a Whip Yank on the rung next to the gate to open it, you don't want to attract their attention, so instead look upward in the flooded room for a pole you can attach your whip to and climb up, and then use the chandelier to swing to the other side to open a gate on the second level.

Here you'll not only have a better vantage point as you return to the Warrior Giant's Tomb, but you'll also find a few Improvised Weapons on the ledge. This is good, as fascists have now overrun the tomb where the tractor fell in on top of where the coffin used to be.

Once again, you don't need to beat up everyone here, and if you want to sneak out, the best way to do so is to avoid the tag team patrols and stick to the far left wall as the patrols move in the opposite direction.

You can use the Improvised Weapons as distractions, and skirt around the walls. Be sure to also look along the left wall for a passage leading down, and you'll find a connecting path to a gate you can open by putting a bust on a pedestal. This leads back to the other big room full of Blackshirts as a shortcut in case you need to re-explore the area later.

Look for a small stairs that head up along the left wall, putting you near the fallen tractor and the scaffolding behind it. There's only a single guard posted nearby watching the tractor, and you can toss a weapon near him to get him to look away.

Whether you distract or knock him out, take this opportunity to make a break for the tractor, and lash your whip to the scaffolding above to pull yourself up. Even if they spot you climbing up, they won't be able to follow.

From here, you'll find additional scaffolding leading back to the Excavation Yard above at the edge of the Apostolic Palace, and the sunlight has never looked so good.

You'll finally be free of the Underworld, but before you can make your next stop at the Fountain of Confession, Indy will decide to follow a sneaky looking Nun.

❖ *Follow the Nun*

Head out of the dig site by climbing up the nearby ladders, and move over to where you saw the nun disappear. A sketch of her will automatically be added into your Journal.

Be sure to unlock the side door that you may have seen earlier leading back into the Apostolic Palace, and check around the storage in this room to find a Shangai Article.

Take the stairs all the way up out of this room, leading to a Clerical Door you can unlock with your key (Indy should automatically put back on his Clerical Suit disguise).

Unfortunately, this small chapel room is full of Nuns, making finding the suspicious one a little tricky. At the very least, snap a photo of the Chapel Altar at the end of the room, and then turn around to spot a Priestess Card on one of the front pews.

In truth, the person you seek has stepped out onto the balcony, so exit through the door to find your quarry, only to be interrupted by the arrival of a giant German airship.

When Indy swipes the binoculars, pan upward along the steps to see Father Ventura and Mussolini himself meeting with the head of the Nazi's occult research program: Emmerich Voss.

You'll learn that the nun is really an investigative journalist named Ginetta Lombardi, tracking down the whereabouts of her missing sister. She'll slip in a Photograph of Laura and makes a deal with you to trade info should either of you find anything of use.

❖ *Bring the Parchment to Antonio*

While you're still on the balcony, take a snapshot of the airship, and then look for a zipline to take you out of here to a nearby roof ledge. Once you land, you should be right in front of an Adventure Book, Fruit Bag.

Get the Blackshirt's Disguise

Before leaving the area, look back through the chainlink fence for an area below where several thugs are out of uniform at a Washing Tent, and a nice clean uniform is just lying out in open. There's a gap in the fence you can crawl through.

Drop down to beat up the group, and then loot the place for all it's worth, including the Blackshirt Uniform, Medicine Bottle on a bench, a small breakable lockbox, plus a photo of the Washing Tent and another Strange Inscription that Antonio is looking for!

The Blackshirt Uniform will allow you move through restricted areas without getting hassled (unless a Captain is around) and even has a key for certain locked areas.

Head down the stairs from the rooftops to find yourself back in the Borgia Courtyards, and then make a beeline for Antonio at the Apostolic Library. Show the parchment that the Warrior Giant's skeleton had on it, and your next destination will be clear - The Fountain of Confession.

❖ Investigate the Fountain

The Fountain is located off in the southwest of the city, south of the Blackshirt Barracks up a ramp past where a Captain is inspecting his troops.

Before you head off, Indy mentions this might be a good time to wrap up any loose ends, so feel free to chase down any other Fieldwork you haven't finished, including a new update from Gina that gets added as the Nun in Trouble Fieldwork, and also try using your Blackshirt Uniform to check out some camps and the Underground Boxing Ring by the Borgia Courtyards.

You can of course revisit The Vatican later in your Adventure, but it's a good bet you won't be able to do any fast traveling back for at least a little while.

When you're ready, head west from the Belvedere Courtyard and slip up the ramp south of the Blackshirt Barracks by dodging around the Blackshirt Captain inspecting his troops.

The large fountain will come into view, with a large stone dragon in the middle up a series of steps. Be sure to check around the truck for a Military Ration Chest, and then head up the stairs, and snap a photo of the fountain.

Indy will need a way to get inside the fountain, and the only entrance seems to be a small gate on the left that's locked. There are also two inscriptions at the base of each "tower" you can take photos of. One mentions a "dragon of light must turn to the dark" and the other says a "dark beast looked upon the light".

Luckily, there's another Military Ration Chest nearby that just so happens to hold a Fountain Gate Key you can use on the gate nearby.

Before heading on, check around near the back of the flatbed truck for a small lockbox you can break open for money, and then head up far steps to the left. Here you'll find what should be the final Strange Inscription that Antonio was looking for (if you return to give him all the photos, you'll get an Ancient Artifact in return!).

With the gate key in hand, open up the gate, and use your whip to rappel up the old scaffolding to the top floor where you can swing back across to end up on the balcony.

You'll be next to the dragon lit up by the sunlight, and it seems to be missing its claw Look down below on the scaffolding, and you can spot the claw on a red blanket. As you grab it, Indy will be surprised by the arrival of Gina.

When you get back to your feet, climb back up and place the Dragon Claw on the statue, and rotate it so that a bar extends from it.

The inscription below the tower read that the dragon of light needed to turn to the dark, so rotate the statue so that it faces toward the middle.

Next, swing across to the far dragon (which thankfully has its claw still attached), and rotate the claw to extend another pole, and rotate this one to "face the light" toward the middle.

This will cause the statue in the middle of the fountain to turn around, and reveal a small rung you can yank with your whip, and in doing so will reveal a large inner area of the fountain, as well as a large new puzzle to solve if you want to get inside.

❖ *The Fountain of Confession Puzzle*

A large rectangular block will rotate around, showing diorama sculptures on three sides before stopping to face you with three figures in front of a sealed gate. You'll need to solve the puzzles on both sides of this sculpture to gain entry. Take a photo of the entrance first.

Drop down into the fountain and pull the large lever that has appeared with Gina, which will rotate the sculpture again to the first main puzzle.

You'll encounter a baptism scene, with a child on the left, and a man gathering water on the right. Take a photo of the scene, which you can take more photos of for hints.

You can move this diorama around by pulling various lever, but the order is the Key:

1. Push the praying boy in the basin to the right.

2. Use your whip to yank on the rung to deposit water below.

3. Push the man with the bucket left to upend it over the boy.

When done correctly, the statue on the far left will be splashed with water, and a pillar will lower as the sculpture rotates back to the sealed gate.

104

Go back to the fountain and pull the big lever with Gina to rotate the sculpture again to a harder puzzle.

A circular sculpture with three slots has a man in a boat on the left side, and you'll need to guide him over to the right by yanking the rung above. Be sure to snap its photo, and do it more times if you need hints.

However, wooden blocks along the center of the circle block his progress, and you'll need to rotate the three sections of the circle to cause the wooden blocks to drop down and out of the way. You can move Indy's grip up and down to rotate the outer, middle, or inner circle, but If the wooden blocks stick through more than one section then more circles may be moved.

It's a little tricky to solve if you mess up a few times, but this is generally how you can solve it:

1. Rotate the middle and outer circle all the way to the bottom so that the wooden block falls down out of the puzzle.

2. Rotate the outer circle so that the openings form a "T" for the boat to get through.

3. Rotate the middle circle so that the opening form a "T" for the boat to get through.

4. Rotate the inner circle with the last wooden block to form a "T" so that the block drops down, freeing a path for the boat to move to the right.

Once the way is clear, yank the right ring with your whip to move the boat along, and the puzzle will be solved.

As the structure moves back to the front, you can now push the child statue in the middle, causing the gate to open, and a staircase to form down into the Courtyard Underground!

❖ *The Fountain Underground*

Head down the spiral staircase to find a strange underground area, and a walkway

105

with what seems to be fire beneath you -- it won't hurt to walk on it.

Follow Gina to find a large lever, and pull it to light up the area, revealing a large statue you can take a photo of for more clues.

Heed well the warning about the trials, as Indy takes a few steps into the next passageway to fall right into a pit. Oops.

Luckily, the pool of what seems to be oil hasn't been set ablaze, and you can move to the left to find a path into the First Trial.

❖ Chamber of Tribulations

As you enter the large room, looking above you'll find giant swinging pendulum blades, and some low ledges you can climb up to reach Gina. Take a photo of the scary blades, then steel yourself for the trial.

There's no secret to this one, just plain courage and timing. Jump across the first to platforms and stop, waiting for the blade to swing left before jumping across to the long central platform.

Secret - Ancient Relic

Before you take on the second part of the chamber, note that this area also has a separate pool of oil below. Drop down into it, and look on a ruined small platform for an Ancient Relic you can grab.

This section has two working pendulum blades, and you'll need to step onto the first ledge and time your first jump carefully, then race across the second thin platform to dodge the last blade.

Gina will follow at her own pace, and together you can step forth into the giant Monastery Courtyard. This impressive area features a giant ominous door backed by angels, with two giant dragons holding shields on either side. Snap a photo of the Ornamented Gate, and then look up behind you for a path.

Up the stairs behind where you entered, you'll find two giant stone objects you can ignore for the moment, and two large levers. Pulling each lever will cause the dragon statues to move their shields aside to reveal two paths, which the Courtyard Plaque between them will reveal more info about.

To advance through the doors, you'll need to forge two sacred keys by completing challenges of silver and gold. Both dragons lead to a challenge for their respective color, and we'll take the Silver Dragon on the left first.

❖ *Silver Path Trial Puzzle*

Taking the path through the Silver Dragon leads to a room bathed in red light. Be sure to look for another Silver Path Plaque to take a picture of before moving into the central room.

The middle of the room features a large slab that seems to hold some kind of

107

receptacle, and large vents with fire below are on each side.

Ahead, there's a sealed door, but you can look to the left to find a skeleton in a barred room holding a Stone Tablet.

Return to the center and place this tablet in the receptacle, and the trial will spring to life. Now the grates below will start to burn you if you walk over them, but luckily there are poles on either side.

Look left from the receptacle where you placed the tablet, and swing across to a far platform with another Stone Tablet.

However, Indy can't swing and hold the tablet at the same time, but luckily Gina will be on the other side of the bars to grab it for you. Unluckily, when you try to swing back, the pole will break.

Things are only getting hotter now, but you can look on the opposite side of the platform for a fallen pillar leaning against a wall, and jump up to carefully shimmy along the ledge.

Keep moving to the side until you are safely over the middle platform before dropping down, and then swing over to the far side.

Grab the Stone Tablet back from Gina, and place it in the receptacle to open the door

The fires won't exactly die out, but you shouldn't wait around, and swing back over to race through the door and complete the trial!

Heading up the stairs from the Silver Trial, you'll come to a large area that looks like a forge, which you can take a photo of.

Pull the chain in the middle of the forge and don't be afraid when everything blazes to life around you.

Instead, hop off the forge and go into the next room to watch the molten lava being poured into the mold for a key. Once the lava is in, yank the rung above with your whip to cool it with water, and carry the Silver Key to the large door. Next up, the Gold Trial.

On the path through to the Gold Trial, you'll find a long hall with a sealed gate at the end. Look left, and you can spot a small hole in the wall to crawl through. Look for a statue bust to place on a pedestal in this area, which will unlock the gate outside.

Head through, and you'll find an Ancient Artifact here.

❖ *Gold Path Trial Puzzle*

Pull on the chain when you reach the next room to open up the Gold Trial room. As with the Silver Trial, you should take a photo of the Gold Trial Plaque for more clues.

Light is supposed to guide your path here, but there's nothing matching that so far, just large hanging pillars over circular grates with fires below. If you try to pull the lever at the end of the room, you'll just get burned a little bit.

To start solving this puzzle, look for a small side room with more chains to pull on, and you'll find that each chain moves one of the pillars along the circular grates. One of these grates will light up with fire when the pillar crosses over it.

There are only two chains to work with here, so pull the farthest pillar to the second grate from the far wall, and the chain next to it all the way so that pillar is as close to you as possible.

This doesn't seem to be enough to solve the puzzle, but you may notice an open section of wall high up. A little to high for you to reach.

111

Check the pillar you pulled alongside the other wall, and look up to find a pole you can reach from this height. Climb up a bit on your whip, and then swing to a rung on the pillar to hold on.

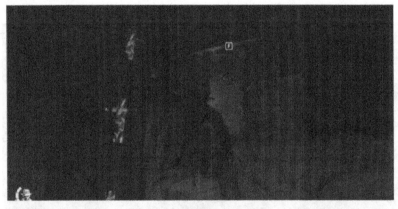

Gina will helpfully pull the pillar to the far side of the room, allowing you to swing through the opening in the wall, putting you on the side with the remaining chains to move the last few pillars under a grate that light ups.

There are five circular grates on each row, with four rows in total. When you're done, it should look like this:

Entrance				
			X	
	X			
				X
		X		
Lever				

When you are certain all four pillars have a lit fire under them, return to the lever, and this time the door will open, completing the trial.

As with the other trial, repeat the steps of finding the Gold Forge (and taking a picture), pulling the chain to light up the forge, head back into the courtyard, and douse the lava in the mold to gain the Gold Key.

With both keys forged, place them both in the large door, and the way open to this secret hall will finally be revealed!

❖ *Secret Monastery*

You'll finally have reached the hiding place of a mysterious Vatican Ancient Order, and closer than ever to finding your stolen Cat Mummy. First, you'll need to start looking for clues.

Start by snapping a photo of the giant Metatron Statue in the center of the Monastery, and then look or a doorway to the left.

Look for a way up some stairs to reach the second floor, and you'll find a door at the end that's locked. Luckily, you have Gina and her lockpicking skills to open the way.

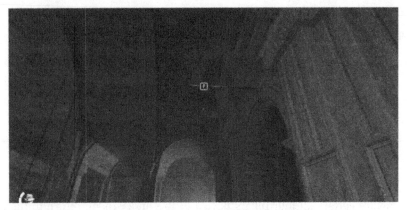

Before following Gina into the room she unlocks, look for a broken part of the balcony to use your whip to swing across to the far side.

Explore the length of this far balcony, and you can find an Atonement Prayer Adventure Note at the edge.

Inside the Scriptorium, you'll find a large plethora of notes and books. Check the books on the right as you enter to read the History of the Crusades and a Biblia Sacra Cover. Gina will find a mug nearby... it's still warm.

On the far side of the room, you'll find two more books that will trigger some short cutscenes - the Secrets of the Christian Church, and the opposite side an Unknown Language Book alongside a Strange Writing Page, and Junia's Prayers for Atonement.

Finally, read the small letter mentioning a "Brother Locus" who traveled to obtain your stolen Cat Mummy, which has been stashed in the Treasury of Esoteric Artifacts.

Gina, meanwhile, has been inspecting a portrait of a Pope, and has found it to be a secret panel you can help her open. Not a moment too soon, as someone seems to be following you.

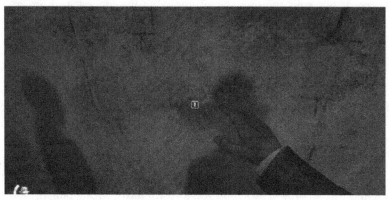

The Secret Passage may look to be a dead end, until Gina notices a symbol on the wall you can wipe away to reveal its the same one you found in library, meaning you can use the Giant's Pendant on it.

Opening this secret door, you'll find yourself entering this fabled Treasury of Esoteric Artifacts. What a find!

While you unfortunately can't grab everything here, Indy can at least take a photo of the treasury, to preserve its memory at the very least.

Have fun looking around at all the crazy artifacts from all over the world. Eventually, Gina will point out your missing Cat Mummy, sitting among a group of similar looking idols.

Unfortunately, no sooner do you take hold of it, than the very same Cat Mummy Thief returns to demand you put it back. Time for a rematch.

❖ Boss Fight - Brother Locus

Hopefully you've found enough Medicine Bottles to buy a health or stamina upgrade or two from Sister Valeria, because Brother Locus still hits very hard. Similarly, having food on hand to give yourself some temporary extra points can't hurt either.

As you might expect, the giant is a tough nut to crack, has a strong defense, and can grab you to deal a lot of damage. Your Whip won't really do much either, and don't try to pull him with it, or he'll just yank you forward into a strong punch.

116

Instead, play this one very slow and carefully. You can try to shove, but more often than not his guard is very hard to break. You can try and break through with a charged heavy hit of your own, but don't waste all your stamina and leave yourself open.

Instead, wait for him to drop his guard and unleash either a grab or heavy attack and dodge to the side, then retaliate with a few quick jabs or a big hit of your own, then fall back to dodge the next attack.

If he grabs you, mash to get out and retreat to wait for your health to regenerate a little bit.

Gina will try throwing things at him, and in doing so can become an unlikely MVP. Though the items she tosses don't seem to do much, it can actually cause Locus to turn and focus his attention on her.

The moment his attention is off you, that's your cue to unload with a flurry of punches to take advantage of his lack of guard, and then back off when he turns back to face you.

Keep this up, and wait for Gina to provide you openings, and the giant will finally fall to his knees, where one last punch can KO the big guy.

Since things rarely go as planned, Father Venture will choose this moment to allow Mussolini and his new friend Emmerich Voss to access the treasury, as Indy and Gina narrowly find a hiding place.

You'll finally get to learn about the truth behind the Cat Mummy's true value, and what Voss wants with it and relics like it: The Great Circle. The scene will end as they leave. Time to chase some Nazis.

⬧ *Follow the Nazis*

Gina will dash off to unlock a nearby door, so quickly follow her into one last room of the Treasury.

This room should hold your final Adventure Notes, including a Ziggurat Dig Report in the left corner, Rossi's Letter along a small wall in the center, and an Artifacts List alongside the final Ancient Artifact you can find in The Vatican!

When you're ready to head out, help Gina unlock the last door with the Giant's Pendant, and you'll leave this area behind.

❖ *Rooftop of St. Peter's Basilica*

You'll find yourself at the top of a Vatican Basilica now, where the German Airship is preparing to leave. Gina will run off ahead, forcing you to find an alternate way up. The path is short, but it does get a little dangerous.

To start, wait for the lift to go up before swinging forward, and then leap down to a wooden platform below.

Head left along the basilica by jumping across the gaps, and then swing off the crane to the top of another lift and up to a crane.

Shimmy along the scaffolding here moving right until you can pull yourself up, where you should find two windows. Take the right one by using your whip to pull yourself up, and you'll enter a crawlspace below some stairs.

Climb up the scaffolding here to a ledge, but be wary, as a Nazi Officer is patrolling near. If he hears you and tries to investigate, drop back down and lure him to the ledge, and you can yank him off with your whip.

A note about Nazis: Unlike the Blackshirts, they aren't opposed to using guns. If you have Improvised Weapons, strike hard and fast, and don't give them time to draw their guns, or otherwise disarm them fast with your whip.

You can sneak down the stairs to beat up the other Nazi at the bottom, or continue heading up to find a third Nazi to smack, and the fourth at the very top of the stairs. Speed and power will be key if they spot you trying to sneak up.

When you reach the door, another scene will play out as the Nazis prepare to leave. Indy will get caught by a familiar snake in the grass, but the arrival of a former adversary gives him time to latch onto the airship with his whip.

When you get control back, shimmy across the airship to find a hatch you can open, and Gina will try to pull you in. When she fails the first time, climb back up with your whip and she'll get it right the second time.

You'll be heading for Gizeh next, which is a good time for Indy to brief Gina all about what The Great Circle is, and why they need to find it before Voss does. The Race is On!

SIDE QUESTS

A SAVAGE DISCOVERY WALKTHROUGH

- Reward: 300 Adventure Points
- Related Notes: 4

This Fieldwork Sidequest can be started as soon as you are able to leave the Apostolical Library in Vatican City, either by finding the archaeologist, or getting clued into the quest by finding a special note.

You can find this note in the first Blackshirt tent as you exit the library, and search for a clipboard that has a Theft Report on it, mentioning the archaeologist's assistant being confined.

You'll find Professor Savage himself in the alleys behind the Borgia Courtyard, by a notice board leading up to the restricted Apostolical Palace entrance. The British archaeologist is clad entirely in white and hard to miss with his constant complaining.

Lend an ear, and he'll mention that his assistant had found a stone tablet which may have provided a clue to the "fallen angels" that Indy has been looking into. However, only the assistant knows what happened to the tablet, and he's now confined in a Blackshirt campsite under guard.

119

Before you head off, be sure to look on a barrel opposite the professor to find a small Fool Playing Card note related to the fieldwork.

Rescue Sidney

The archaeologist's assistant Sidney is being held in a Blackshirt camp to the northwest, north along the street above the Borgia Courtyard bordering the Vatican Gardens. As you might expect, it's incredibly restricted, so you'll have to do some sneaking to get the job done (we don't recommend getting into any prolonged fights, especially with the amount of guards both in and outside the camp).

To get in without raising any alarms, carefully skirt around the Captain inspecting his troops by the large door back to Belvedere Courtyard, and look for a series of scaffolding to the right of the Blackshirt camp.

Avoid using your whip to climb while in sight of any thugs, and instead take a ladder up and then climb to the highest ledge. Move alongside the scaffolding until you can spot a zipline, which is placed in just the right position to send you into one the higher up tents in the camp.

Crouch and stay hidden once you land, and be sure to investigate the room for Lira to swipe, and a Medicine Bottle for the A Remedy For All Discovery Quest.

There is a stairway down here, but it leads to a locked door, so instead you'll need to take the top floor route. The next room has two Blackshirts, but one stays in his desk chair while the other alternates looking out a window and standing against a wall. Wait for him to look out the window before clobbering him with an Improvised Weapon, then do the same for the guy in the chair who refuses to look around.

Be sure to stash these bodies in the next room, as another Blackshirt from the floor below may patrol up the stairs and stumble across the bodies.

Once they've been moved, look on the table by the stairs down to grab a St. Peter Postcard to add to your notes, then cautiously sneak down the stairs.

At the bottom of the stairs is the holding cell, but it's guarded by a heavy bruiser that's hard to get the drop on. You can try tossing a bottle by the locked door to get him to look away from the stairs, or just rush in with an Improvised Weapon and hit him hard and fast.

Once the guard is down, look by the desk for a Jail Cell Key hanging on the wall, and use it to unlock the cell next to you. Note that there's also a padlock box here you can break with a weapon to score even more loot!

After getting mistakenly ambushed by Sidney, he'll relay to you that the stone tablet was taken by a worker named Giuseppe over at the dig site.

Find Giuseppe at the Excavation Site

Once Sidney has run off, you'll want to carefully lure out the Blackshirts in the adjoining room if you haven't already (you can also use the stairs) and then loot the building and all of its lockers for any other Lira they have stashed away.

To find an easy way out of the barracks, look for another room to the left as you exit the cell area, and you'll find a hatch between two beds.

Drop and crouch down to move beneath the barracks, and you'll be shielded by the wooden walls. Simply follow the route straight to find an exit along some shrubs that will shield your escape, and then bypass the Captain as you leave.

To get to the Excavation Site at the Apostolic Palace, you'll need to find a good route inside. There's actually quite a few, depending on what other side quests you are working on or if you want to be louder or quiet.

The main entrance to the Apostolic Palace can be found by traveling from the Borgia Courtyard outside the Sistine Chapel along the pathway east, where you'll find a checkpoint manned by more than a few guards. Luckily, there's a nearby way to circumvent this.

Head back down the path and look for an entrance into a chapel that's draped over and under renovation. There's only workers and priests here, so they won't mind you utilizing your whip to scale the scaffolding and swing across the chandelier.

While you're here, be sure to also snap a photo of the Window Cleaning up on the top level to add to your notes.

At the top of the scaffolding, you can exit onto a roof, and climb up to the right to see a high window above where the guarded entrance was.

Entering through this window will put you on the second floor, which unfortunately has its share of Blackshirts patrolling around. One is likely down the stairs where you need to go, while another is right around the corner guarding a secondary window exit, while two more are on the far side of the upper floor balcony.

If you're looking to catalogue more Notes however, you may have to engage the two other Blackshirts on the second floor.

Once they're down, snap a photo of the Vatican Seal on the ceiling, and then check the far end of the second floor balcony for a red couch with an Ipeo Card for your notes. If you head into the room they were guarding, you can also uncover a new Mystery. Should you exit through the top floor window, you'll also have the correct view to snap a photo of the Vatican Excavation.

Otherwise, you can quietly head down the stairs and make a right to a grand stairwell, and cross to the other side to find another exit to the Excavation Yard.

There are a lot of people working the yard, and finding Guiseppe may prove to be a challenge, so you'd best start with the office building on the far side. Note the two Blackshirts to the left, with a third crossing a wooden walkway to the far side.

They are usually looking away, and you can clobber the nearest one and then inspect the corner of the dig site to find one of the Inscriptions that Antonio is looking for.

Stick to the right, but resist the urge to move all the way to the wall behind the red brick arches, as the back wall is hiding a lot more lounging Blackshirts.

Instead, wait for another to patrol across the wooden ramp closest to you and knock him out before stashing him behind some scaffolding.While there's an Officer guarding the front entrance, you should now have a clear line to quickly sneak into the other door away from the Officer. One of the Blackshirts against the far wall may start to notice, but as long as you enter quickly, he won't follow.

Inside the office, there's a good deal of loot to take for yourself, including a Medicine Bottle at the front entrance, and some Lira both on one of the tables and in a desk drawer below.

The real prizes are at the center L-shaped table - a Dig Site Schedule that lists Guiseppe in zone F. There's also a Swiss Guard Postcard to also add to your notes.

After narrowly avoiding the untimely arrival of Father Ventura himself, you'll now have to go find Guiseppe in the yard below. Luckily, all the zones have large lettering so you can find your way.

Exit out the side leading back the way you came and drop down into the excavated yard, and head down to take a left just as you pass an old bulldozer.

Enter the underground tunnel and look for an orange glow coming from someone working with a lantern around the corner. Speak to the worker and ask for the tablet, but he won't give up that intel without a fight.

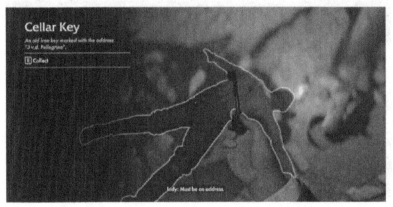

Give them the ol' one-two beatdown to send him to the floor, after which you can check his body for a Cellar Key. It had the address "3 v.d. Pellegrino".

To escape the yard, look for a gate next to the office building you found the schedule in, which you can unlock from this side. The bad news is two Blackshirts are lounging around as you exit, and with nothing better to do, they want to beat you up. Too bad for them.

Once they've taken a seat, head down the stairs and drop down the scaffolding to go past the Tower of Nicholas V and onto Via Di Belvedere. The cellar in question is in a place you may have passed before: It's on the side of the Vatican Post Office building.

Go up the side street near the checkpoint, and look for stairs going down to where a giant 3 is marked above a door. Use your key to get inside.

As you enter, the Stone Fragment will be right in front of you on a pile of rubble against the far wall.

After checking it out, you'll be interrupted by another Blackshirt, who will need to pay for his crimes against antiquity.

Before you leave, be sure to check the far corner of this room for another one of the Inscriptions that Antonio wants a picture of, along with a locked chest.

With the Stone Tablet in hand, you'll find Professor Savage and Sidney back at the Apostolic Library.

They've taken up residence at a table on the first floor, and you'll find they've left an Adventure Book here for the Marshall College Guide, which will help you track down any notes from there you may have missed. You can also take a photo of the Teacher and Apprentice with your camera to add a new note.

Hand over the tablet, and the quest will be complete.

THE MAD PRIEST WALKTHROUGH

- Reward: 225 Adventure Points
- Related Notes: 6

This Fieldwork Sidequest can be started after reaching the Vatican Post Office during your adventure to find a Camera, and can either be triggered by finding a relevant note in the Post Office, or speaking to Sister Catherine directly.

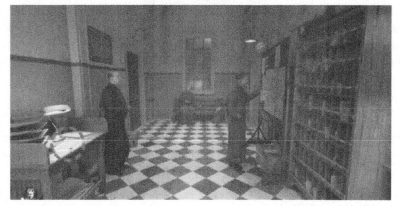

You can find this note in the Vatican Post Office hallway outside the Janitor's Room, where a slightly crumpled Catherine's Letter can be found to trigger the sidequest.

You'll find Sister Catherine herself in the Sistine Chapel, which is located southwest of Belvedere Courtyard, and can be quickly accessed by opening the large doors heading west to the Vatican Gardens and then south along the street toward the Borgia Courtyard. The entrance is just past the signpost for the chapel, and requires a Clerical Key to enter.

While you're here, be sure to snap a photo of the Sistine Chapel Ceiling with your camera.

Speak with the grumbling Sister Catherine to learn that Antonio was supposed to send her a diary of the mad Father Crescenzo by way of a delivery boy. Considering how integral his notes are to your own adventure, it's worth seeing if you can get any intel out of this journal yourself before handing it over, and so Indy will volunteer to go get it.

Before you leave, you can also snap a photo of Sister Catherine herself to add to your notes.

Unfortunately, when you return to the Apostolical Library to check in on Antonio, you'll find Father Ventura has beaten you to the punch, and confiscated a number of books in Antonio's possession... which includes the diary.

Antonio believes the confiscated material is likely kept in a secure section of the Apostolical Palace, which is not only under heavy guard, but locked up as well. Luckily, he knows of a secret entrance through the sewers beneath the Tower of Nicholas V, and will give you the Sewer Key to access it.

Before you go, check Antonio's desk to find Ventura's Letter that the Man in Black has left behind, and add it to your sidequest notes.

Infiltrate the Apostolical Palace Through the Sewers

To reach the part of the palace where the diary has been taken, you'll need to take a specific route. Travel down Belvedere Courtyard to Via Di Belvedere, all the way to the entrance to the Tower of Nicholas V.

Once inside, stick to the right of the interior to find a stairway down leading to the Sewers area. You can also snap a photo of the Sewer Bridge to add to your notes.

Using the Sewers Key, unlock the gate next to the bridge and dozing Blackshirt guard, and proceed onward to find a large open cistern that looks like a dead end.

Cross the bridge on the far side of the room, and look next to some piping for some white scuff marks that indicate you can grab onto a wooden ledge built over the pipes. Climb to the right, and then upward along a pipe, and then right again until it breaks free and creates an extra section of pipe to shimmy across.

Once you reach the edge, look up for several pipes hanging from a rope in the middle of the cistern, and latch on with your Whip to grab onto the pipe on the far side. Climb up and over to reach a ledge, and then whip to a higher ledge before climbing up the Whip.

Finally, use your whip on the pipe just below the ceiling grate to swing across to the far side, and climb up the ledge to exit the cistern.

As you climb up here, you'll find one of the Strange Inscriptions to snap a photo of for Antonio's Fieldwork quest, The Secret of Giants.

At the top, you'll find a gate to unlock with a shortcut to the rampart leading back to Castel Sant'Angelo, and another path leading up some stairs into the Apostolic Palace — as well as a Medicine Bottle to recover for Sister Valeria's quest.

At the top of the stairs, you'll find a Clerical Door leading into a restricted storage area of the Apostolic Palace (Indy will automatically don his Clerical Suit in this area though you will still be attacked on sight).

Luckily, you don't have far to look for the missing journal. As you enter, look for a low table to the right with a red military rations crate you can open, and the journal will be right there for the taking!

While you're in this restricted room, you may as well do a bit of extra exploring. Look around one of the central stacks of stored items to find a Confiscation Manifest Note alongside an Adventure Book for Iron Grip 1.

Then, step into the middle of the room and look back at that area with your camera to snap a photo of the Stolen Artifacts.

Try not to linger too long, as there's a good chance a bulky Blackshirt Goon may come in through the far door to the rest of the palace to patrol around. However, if you're also on the side quest A Savage Discovery, you'll find yourself right next to the excavation site, should you need to sneak in there.

To escape this area, you can head through the door opposite the one leading to the dig site, and unlocking this door leads to a rooftop exit with a sleeping guard, letting you drop back down onto Via Di Belvedere.

Return to the Sistine Chapel to drop off the diary now that you've had your fill, and you'll be waylaid by Father Ventura, who has a warning for you before the quest concludes and you earn your Adventure Points.

A NUN IN TROUBLE FIELDWORK WALKTHROUGH

How To Get Into the Museum

To start the quest, follow Gina from the Cistine Chapel and head out into the main courtyard. She'll leave you behind, so head to where the objective marker is.

At one end of the main courtyard is a restricted area surrounded by a fence and guards. You have two options to get in.

- Use the Blackshirt disguise to be let in without alerting the enemies.

- Sneak into the area.

You get the Blackshirt disguise from the area underneath where you first met Gina, by some washing areas for the Nazis. You use a zipline that leads from the Apostolic area. After going down the zipline, turn around and head though a gap in the fence, and drop down to the washing area. After knocking out the goons, the disguise is on the chair.

You'll also get the Blackshirt Key alongside the disguise, which is really useful for unlocking locked doors around the Vatican.

To sneak in, there's a gap in the fence to the left of the restricted area when you're looking at the door to the Vatican's library, where you go to get to Antonio's office. There's also a gap to shimmy through on the opposite side, by the wall to the outside of the courtyard, next to some wooden crates.

Follow the path through there and up some stairs in the Vatican museum courtyard. Gina will be there with an open window for you to climb through. Now, follow the path around until you get into the museum itself.

Art Room And Museum

Once you reach the art room, you need to find clues about what happened to Giuliana. Those are:

- Blood on the wall.
- A piece of cloth on the floor in the corner below.
- An ID card between the two paintings.
- A note on a box by a lantern.

Gina will then give you a photo of yourself before she picks the lock on the next door. Then, head down the stairs and you'll see footprints in white paint. Take a picture of the blood in the next room and there will be a gold ring in it for you to pick up.

You now need to fight or avoid the Nazis who arrive, then continue on through the rooms and back to the main Vatican courtyard.

You're now looking for Borgia Tower, which is the one with the big Mussolini poster in front of it. Head over there and climb up to the open window by heading around the back of the poster and using your whip to climb up the scaffolding.

Head right and Gina will open the door to the tower for you. Next, avoid or defeat the enemies and start heading up the tower via a ladder in the middle of the room.

You'll encounter a locked door, so grapple with the whip to your right and swing over. Head up and you'll be able to squeeze through a gap on your left, then follow round and you'll drop into a room the other side of the locked door on the floor below.

Just remove the blockage for Gina and keep heading up, defeating more bad guys on your way.

Finding Giuliana

Once you reach the top of the tower, Gina will then pick another lock and you'll need to fight a more powerful nazi. After you've knocked him out, take the ties off Giuliana's feet, and a cutscene will play.

You'll then complete the quest and be given Giuliana's key, which opens a door a couple of floors lower in the Borgia Tower. That leads to the tricky Father and Son Mystery quest.

Note: Giuliana's Key only opens two doors in the tower, but it'll stay in your inventory until you use it.

VOSS' GOLD STASH FIELDWORK WALKTHROUGH

Getting Into The Camp

Actually getting into the camp without being caught is probably the toughest part of the Fieldwork quest. Once you've made your way to the right area, you need to pick a way to enter the place that's swarming with bad guys.

Instead of taking the obvious choice, which involves the big bridge that acts as a front gate, head to the right side of the camp and leave your boat a little way off from the area.

Then, creep around the right-hand side of the camp, not actually entering it, until you're on the far right corner of it, right by the scaffolding at the back.

From there, you can jump up onto the structure and avoid most of the Nazis who will attack on sight. Then, head into the large office room from the door at the back of the camp. Be careful, as there are three armed guards in here. You can either take them out loudly or creep past them and go up the stairs on one side of the room.

In there, you'll encounter a captain you need to take out quietly, as well as a locked safe.

Don't take out the captain with guns, as you'll alert the guards that still litter the camp, including those in the room below you. You won't be alive for long if you make too much noise.

Opening Voss' Safe And Getting Gold Bars

Once you've knocked the captain out, you'll be able to grab the combination instructions from his body, allowing you to open the safe.

The note he has says that the code is **5484**, so open the safe using it. Inside, you'll find four gold bars worth a total of $2,000.

Be sure to take a picture of Voss' camp from the balcony before you leave to get those bonus Adventure Points.

You can now head back to Gina and the vendor to buy the Rebreather and carry on with the main quest.

ELEPHANT IN THE ROOM WALKTHROUGH

How To Start The Elephant In The Room Mystery

You'll find this mystery in the far back corner of Voss's Camp, near the location of the Royal Army Disguise, and behind the building where the A Game of Wits mystery is found. Just past the large green tent, you'll find a staircase leading down towards the left. There are two enemies here standing under a white tent that will ignore you if you're wearing the Royal Army Disguise. Take a picture of the Elephant Statue and head inside where the Elephant in the Room mystery awaits.

To begin the quest, take a picture of the Buddhist Statue.

How To Solve The Elephant In The Room Puzzle

To solve this puzzle you'll need to find three elephant statuettes and place them into the three slots underneath the Buddhist statue. There are a series of platforms that open and close different doors in this shrine, so you'll need to move your available statuettes around a lot to find the solution.

To start, take your lighter over to the left and burn the false wall. Your first elephant statuette is behind it. Bring this statue over to the Buddhist statue and place it in the slot on the right. This will open a secret door to another pedestal on the statues right.

Next, grab the second statuette out of the cubby on the right wall. Place this one on the newly revealed pedestal on the wall to the right of the Buddist statue. This will open up the left slot underneath the Buddhist statue.

Next, you need to take the first statuette out of the right slot under the Buddhist statue and move it to the left slot. This will open a secret passageway on the left side of the statue.

Inside the secret passageway, grab the Rebel Journal on the ground near the entrance. It turns out the rebels were using these ruins as a hideout before the General invited Voss and the Nazis in.

At the end of this room, you'll find a map to the Sukhothai Relics.

Next, turn the corner and you'll find a broken staircase against the left wall. Ascend as high as you can, and then look straight up to find a grapple point. If you get a bit of a running start and jump, you can throw your whip at the height of your jump and latch onto this grapple point. Climb your rope about halfway, then swing and jump onto the ledge ahead of you. You'll find the third elephant at the top.

Now, you can leave this secret passageway, but before you do, make a note of the pedestal on the left as you exit. Placing a statuette here will reveal the middle pedestal under the Buddhist statue in the main room.

Now it's time to juggle the statuettes until you get all three onto the three pedestals. Here are the steps to get all three into position.

1. Place the third elephant on the right pedestal under the Buddhist Statue to reveal the second elephant on the pedestal to the right of the statue.

2. Bring the second elephant into the secret passageway and place it on the pedestal on the right near the entrance.

3. Take the third elephant off of the right pedestal under the Buddhist Statue and move it to the middle one.

4. Retrieve the second elephant from the pedestal inside the secret passageway and place it on the right pedestal under the Buddhist statue.

With all three elephant statutes in position, another secret passageway will open on the righthand wall. Take a picture of the Elephant Skeleton here to complete the mystery. Before you leave, feel free to grab the shotgun or dynamite if you'd like to get some payback on the fascists waiting outside.

❖ All Mystery Note Locations For Elephant In The Room

Note	Location

Note	Location
Buddhist Statue Photo	Take a picture of the Buddhist statue as you enter the ruins
Rebel Journal	Found on the floor inside the lefthand secret passageway
Elephant Skeleton Photo	Take a picture of the Elephant Skeleton inside the righthand secret passageway

The only note you can miss, Rebel Journal, is also the only note that explains the reason this elephant puzzle exists.

MYSTERY GUIDE

THE BULLS OF BLOOD MYSTERY GUIDE

- Reward: 100 Adventure Points
- Total Notes: 4

This mystery can be activated by finding either of the three Mystery Notes or interacting with the puzzle itself in the castle.

To find it, proceed through the castle to the Courtyard of the Angel, where a guard walks his dog down a long open area with barracks and a garage on one side, and a stone building on the other.

Dart past the guard and his dog while they walk one direction to slip into either one of the doorways. You'll find a guard asleep in a chair in each of the main rooms, with a third Blackshirt patrolling between them and the altar room in the middle.

Look in the room farthest away from the locked gate outside requiring the Captain's Key, and you can find Russo's Note on a table in the middle of the room. It mentions a passage next to a fireplace, but it's not referencing the fireplace in the room you're currently in.

144

Instead, pass through the altar room to the other large room nearest the gate that requires the Captain's Key, and look for the Blackshirt asleep at the desk. You can knock him out of course, but sneaking around him to check both the Red Bulls Card and Angel Courtyard Map shouldn't disturb him.

The map also mentions the secret passage, the bulls card, and points to a corner of the room you're currently in. Look to the right of the fireplace in this room and you can spot a section of wall with a rectangular mural in the shape of a door, between two portraits of bulls with symmetrical heads of two different colors.

Approach the paintings, and you'll be able to interact with them. To solve the puzzle, you'll need to rotate each painting so that the red-colored bull is upright.

Complete the puzzle, and the secret passage will open. You'll find Cesare Borgia's Letter inside (an incredible historical find!) and be awarded 100 Adventure Points for solving the puzzle.

Even better, you can follow the passage upwards to pull a lever, revealing a balcony area with a red military rations crate, which usually holds a good deal of Lira inside. To the left, you can pull on another lever to open a gate, bypassing the need to get the Captain's Key to exit the Courtyard of the Angel.

A FREE SPIRIT

- Reward: 100 Adventure Points
- Total Notes: 5

This mystery can be activated after you have reached the Vatican Post Office causing the restricted zone around the Tower of Nicholas V to be rescinded.

Once you have the camera, look for a message board across from the tower's entrance beyond a Blackshirt checkpoint that has a hand drawn picture of a missing cat. You can't keep the note, but inspecting it and putting it back will start the quest.

Your goal is to take a photo of the missing cat's location, but there are several cats around the area of the Tower of Nicholas V and Via Di Belvedere, which will at least earn you some extra Adventure Points for finding other cats.

146

Head back up the street and turn right where the Pharmacy run by Sister Valeria is. Just beyond her is a small little courtyard with a tree where a cat is resting. This Black and White Cat isn't your target, but snap a photo anyway.

Next, head up towards Belvedere Courtyard, and look for a small dead end alley by the large door that was initially sealed, across from the gate to the garden area.

Be sure to look around the dead end for a small table with a Medicine Vial for the Remedy for All Discovery Quest. Here you'll be able to jump up the low roofs or climb up the pipe to reach the higher rooftops.

Once you're at the top, you'll be face to face with an Orange Cat. Still not the one you need, but a relevant photo to take.

Turn around from this cat, and look for a narrow section of roofing you can walk across to look down over Via Di Belvedere street. Check by a trio of tiny chimneys to find a White Cat and snap a photo.

Next, cross over the roof of the large door through the road below, and jump to the roofs above the garden area leading to the Vatican Museum.

Stay on the rooftops, and across along the roof to the far wall above the entrance to Belvedere Courtyard, and here you'll find the missing cat in question, Signor Smushki!

To quickly get back down, look along the gardens for a series of scaffolding in the far corner. As you drop down, look for a small pulley and a hanging plank that holds one last Brown Cat to snap a photo of.

Return back to the entrance to the Tower of Nicholas V, and inspect the missing cat note once more. Now you can attach the photo you took to let the Bishop know where it is, and be rewarded with 100 Adventure Points.

You can actually find him reunited with his cat later by checking the low rooftop adjacent to the gardens area!

HOUSE OF GOD

This mystery can be activated by either finding a Mystery Note in a small ornate hallway outside the Apostolical Palace behind Belvedere Courtyard, or interacting with the puzzle itself the note is found on.

Due to its location, there are several methods to reach this area, both from Belvedere Courtyard or the Borgia Courtyard, or by unlocking the door on a higher floor of the Apostolical Palace. The easiest way to reach it is by simply traveling to the far end of Belvedere Courtyard, behind the large propaganda stage being built, and climbing up the scaffolding behind it.

Be sure to climb all the way to the top balcony of the highest balcony above the guard, and slip through the window.

Inside the ornate hallway, there's a large model replica of the Basilica, atop which you can pick up a Cleaning Note that begins the mystery.

The note mentions that the model has several secret compartments, and looking at it you can find a lever in the middle of the model that can be moved from side to side.

Move the lever until it is all the way to the right, and you'll hear the noise of a contraption on the side. Look over on the left side, and you'll find that a slot has opened up to reveal a Relief Medallion.

Grab it, and return to the lever and this time push it all the way to the left side. This will open an identical slot on the opposite side of the model, with a slot for the medallion.

Placing the medallion in the slot will open a new compartment back on the left side, below where you found the medallion. Grab the Golden Chalice, and place it in the center of the Basilica model.

This will complete the puzzle, rewarding you with 100 Adventure Points, and uncovering one final compartment with an Adventure Book for Vatican Relics, which will highlight Ancient Relics on your map when viewing it with the Riddles of the Ancients Discovery Quest selected.

SECRET OF SECRETS

- Reward: 100 Adventure Points, Adventure Book
- Total Notes: 3

This mystery can be activated by finding one of two Mystery Notes in the room outside the Sistine Chapel, located at the edge of the Borgia Courtyard to the southwest in the city, which requires a Clerical Key to enter.

After heading up the stairs to the main chapel room, look into the area before the door to find a locked combination safe, and several statues.

Look for a table in the corner across from the safe for Nicoletti's Letter, which gives a clue for how to open the safe: "look to the stars and the saints: Peter with the key, then Paul with the sword."

This clue is only half of what you need to solve this puzzle, so look around on the central table near the safe for a drawer you can open that holds a Planetary Chart. The diagram holds symbols for all the planets (except Pluto) though some symbols and numbers are missing.

To solve this puzzle and unlock the safe, you must search for the two saints mentioned in the letter, and you'll find three statues in the room. Peter can be found in the farthest corner, and after picking up the statue, rotate to look at its base and you'll find two planetary symbols, however they don't quite match anything on the chart. This is because it's the symbol of Mars (4), which has been smudged out.

With this in mind, check the statue of Paul next by the safe, and check the base to find two more symbols: Mercury and Uranus. Though Mercury doesn't have a number listed, it's the first planet, making them (7) and (1).

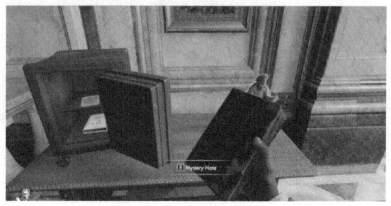

Head to the safe, and using the symbols as a guide, enter 4471 to unlock the safe. Inside you'll find a Cutman 1 Adventure Book, and the other book mentioned in the note. However, it's a forgery, and worthless. The good news is after tossing it aside you can find a Hidden Note under the book that has some spicy info on it, giving you some extra Adventure Points in addition to the 100 you'll get for completing this Mystery.

A SNAKE IN THE GARDEN

This mystery can be activated by finding a Mystery Note in Father Ventura's office — a room of green marble inside the Apostolic Palace's highest floor, overlooking the Excavation Yard.

There are several ways to reach this room, depending on how stealthy or how acrobatic you want to be. The Apostolic Palace can be infiltrated quickly by climbing up to the roofs above the Borgia Courtyards, using the chapel under renovation to swing across the chandelier and climb the scaffolding.

Outside, you'll find the rooftops run across to a high open window leading into the palace.

The top floor of the palace's main room has a long balcony with several Blackshirts guarding the entrance to the office — of which one door is locked from the other side You'll either have to distract the guards or engage several at once to fight your way in

However, you can also look for a window nearby at the top of the stairs that leads onto some scaffolding above the Excavation Yard. There's identical scaffolding on the far side of the yard, and each leads up toward another balcony of Ventura's Office, and you can use your whip to swing over without alerting anyone.

Once inside, look on the main desk for a suspicious Bookcase Note to start the Mystery.

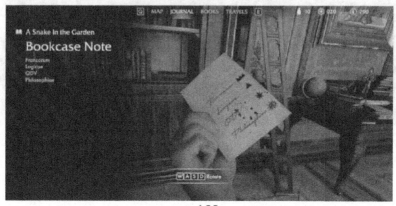

The note mentions a bookcase being redesigned with certain books that "must be taken alphabetically". Flip the card over to see that each title correlates to a symbol:

- Fraoncorum - Crown Symbol
- Logicae - Triangle Symbol
- QDC - Star Symbol
- Philosophiae - Wheel Symbol

Sure enough, the large bookcase in the corner has several large books, and though you can't see the names, the symbols are easily spotted. In order to solve the puzzle, pull out the books in the following order: Crown, Triangle, Wheel, Star.

Done correctly, a compartment will open on the side, revealing a ton of Lira to swipe and a very incriminating Mussolini's Letter to Ventura.

While you have the run of Ventura's office, be sure to also swipe the Medicine Bottle to the right of the bookcase, and take a snapshot of the Dragon Statue.

Be sure to also check the back room for a padlocked box you can smash open to get more money (but be wary of a Blackshirt on duty).

THE HAUNTING MYSTERY GUIDE

How To Start The Haunted Crypt Mystery

This quest begins in the restricted area just north of the Worker's Camp in the southeast corner of the map, close to where you first enter Gizah. The restricted area is the small Nazi camp surrounded by a barbed wire fence. You can enter this area by crawling through a hole in the fence on the back right side, or if you already have the Wehrmacht Uniform from the Knuckle Duster Den quest, you can walk right in the front and the Nazis will ignore you. To start the quest, enter the tent in the middle.

As soon as you enter the tent you'll find three items on the table: a mystery note called Haunting Report, a Tomb Photograph, and a Haunted Tomb Key. The Haunting Report explains that there's a tomb west of the worker's camp that's rumored to be cursed. The entrance has been sealed up, hence the need for the key. Grab all three items and leave the restricted area.

Before leaving the area, don't forget to check the other tent. Inside you'll find some cash, some ammo, and a medicine bottle.

How To Find The Haunted Tomb

If you're near the worker's camp, the entrance to the haunted tomb isn't far. Turn right out of the restricted area and you'll see a red flag in the air, just past the Nazi checkpoint in the road below. That's the marker that will lead you to the tomb entrance.

You'll find the locked gate in a small excavation site just west of the worker's camp. If you picked up the Haunted Tomb Key in the restricted area, you can use it to unlock the gate and enter the tomb. As soon as you open the gate you'll start the hear what sounds like restless spirits moaning in the tomb below. No wonder the Nazis were too afraid to go inside.

158

Of course, it was all a ruse. When you reach the bottom of the tomb you'll find that the sounds are coming from a radio, as well as the Spy's Note, which explains that a spy called 'N' hid a artifact in the tomb and used the ghostly sounds to ward off the Nazis. Grab the note and the nearby Ancient Relic. Reading the note will complete this Mystery. With nothing left to do in this 'haunted' tomb, crawl back out and continue your adventure.

❖ *All Mystery Note Locations For Secret Of Secrets*

Note	Location
Haunting Report	Found in the restricted area near the worker's camp, inside the middle tent.
Tomb Photograph	On the table next to the Haunting Report in the restricted area near the worker's camp
Spy's Note	Inside the Haunted Tomb, requires Haunted Tomb Key.

Like most mysteries, you don't actually need all of the notes to complete this quest. All you need is the Haunted Tomb Key and the Spy's Note you find in the tomb to check this off. Of course, if you find the key it very unlikely you won't find the Haunting Report and Tomb Photograph too, since they're all on the same table.

BRIGHT FUTURE MYSTERY GUIDE

How To Begin The Bright Future Mystery

The note that begins this quest is located in the Nazi Recreation Area, a restricted zone south of the Nazi Compound and west of the Great Sphynx. This is the area where you'll also find the Harvest Stele in a lock box on the bed of a truck. To begin the quest you need to find the note Pohl's Letter. The note is located in an area that's surrounded by fencing and barbed wire. Sneak inside and enter the bigger of the two tents here. In the room at the end where all of the radio equipment is set up, you'll find Pohl's Letter sitting on a table. The letter details a soldier who was caught smuggling stolen equipment along the road to Khentkawes. It directs the recipient to check the soldier's bunk for additional information about his actions, so that's where we'll be heading next.

It is significantly easier to explore this area if you already have the Wehrmacht Uniform from the Knuckle Duster Den questline. If you have this disguise you can walk freely through the restricted areas in Gizah, rather than having to sneak around the Nazis.

Stay in this gated area. You'll find the soldier's bunk in the other big tent here. Carefully cross the courtyard and enter the opposite tent, then examine the rows of bunks against the wall. You'll find the note your looking for on a bottom bunk with a yellow helmet. This is the Nazi Note, and it reveals that the location for the stolen goods is at the mid-point between "the cat" and "the queen", right by the wagon. It also reveals the code to unlock the box, 0926.

Before you leave, open the container on the floor between the two bunks to your left to find the Adventure Book, Brawling - Block Head.

Where To Find The Stolen Goods

If you open your map now you'll find a fairly large search area for the stolen goods. Luckily, we have all the clues we need to narrow it down. Pohl's Letter tells us the soldier was arrested along the road to Khentkawes. On the soldier's bunk, we found a letter that revealed the goods are at the mid-point between "the cat" and "the queen", or in other words, equidistant from the Sphinx and the Khentkawes tomb.

Leave the Nazi Recreational Area and head south towards the Khentkawes dig site. As you make your way there keep an eye out for a few landmarks. You'll see a truck parked in the road with a barrier in front of it. You'll also see a small hill with a makeshift structure covered in red fabric on top of it. The lockbox you're looking for is just to the side of the row between two palm trees, not far from Omar.

Approach the lockbox and enter the code 0926 - but get ready to run! The stash was a trap, and opening it detonates a pile of dynamite hidden inside. Pohl's Letter did mention the soldier was smuggling explosives! Opening the lockbox completes the Bright Future questline.

All Mystery Note Locations For Bright Future

Note	Location
Pohl's Letter	In the big tent within the gated part of the Nazi Recreational Area, on a table covered in radio equipment.
Nazi Note	On a bottom bunk next to a yellow helmet in the gated part of the Nazi Recreational Area, smaller tent.

You may stumble upon the Nazi Note first, in which case you don't necessarily need to find Pohil's Letter to complete this Mystery. For the sake of completion, its worth getting both.

FORTUNE'S REACH MYSTERY GUIDE

How To Find The Trail

After finding the wanted poster, head over to the big wooden tower to the right of the Nawal's tent. Just past that tower, you'll see a smaller tent, and red paint spilled all over the sand from a nearby pot.

Once you've taken a photo of the mess, you'll need to follow the footprints nearby, which start red and quickly turn into just footprints. You'll need to follow those footprints over the road and back towards where you first started when travelling to Gizeh for the first time.

How To Complete Fortune's Reach Mystery

The footprints lead down into a tunnel, where you'll find the missing thieves crushed by falling rocks. Their grave-robbing plan will be in the rocks, and the True Grit book is in the sand.

True Grit is a very useful ability to grab when you can because it sees you take less damage in the last bar of your health. Grab that too while you're awarded Adventure Points for completing the quest.

True Grit is worth getting as soon as possible because it makes you a lot harder to knock out. Each time you're hit on low health, you'll be able to take an extra hit.

COUNTING LETTERS MYSTERY GUIDE

How To Start The Counting Letters Mystery

You'll find this mystery in the restricted area at East Wat Mahathat. You can get here by boat or by fast traveling to the East Wat Mahathat road sign. This is the area with the huge temple where you work with the locals to retrieve this region's stone, but the mystery you're looking for is in a large tent behind the temple to the left.

Getting around this area is much easier if you've already found the Royal Solider disguise in Voss's camp.

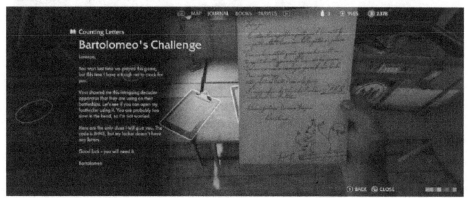

To begin the quest, pick up the note on the table called Bartolomeo's Challenge.

How To Solve The Counting Letters Mystery

As the Bartolomeo's Challenge note explains, you'll need to use the nearby Code Wheels, Code Tables, and Wheel Machine to decode Bartolomeo's code: JHHS.

Your first task is to find the wheels with letters that match the code, but it's not as simple as it first appears. Sort through the four Code Wheels on the ground and you'll find one wheel with a J and an S, two wheels with an H, and one wheel that doesn't have any of the letters you're looking for.

The wheel that doesn't have a J, H, or S on it is a red herring. Throw that one to the side and ignore it. The wheel with a J and an S on it will go in the first and fourth spot in the machine. You'll put it in the first spot first, then after you record the letter move it to the last spot and record its letter too.

As for the two wheels with an H, you'll have to record their letter in both spots. The

163

double letter means there are two possible solutions to this puzzle, but only one code will match the word on the code Table.

To begin, place the code wheel with a J in the first slot of the machine, then each of the wheels with an H in the second and third slot. Leave the fourth slot open for now Close the lid on the machine and rotate the wheels until the top row reads "J H H". The bottom row will read "B I E" or "B E I" depending on which H wheel is on which slot.

Next, open the machine and move the wheel from the first slot into the fourth slot. Then close the machine and rotate the fourth wheel until you see an S in the top row, revealing the bottom letter is an R. You know the code you're looking for is either "BIER" or "BEIR".

Now, pick up the Code Table on the clipboard and look for BIER or BEIR. You'll quickly see that only one of them is on the list. BIER translates to the number 4134. Enter 4134 into the padlock on the chest and open it to complete this mystery.

All Mystery Note Locations For The Counting Letters Mystery

Note	Location
Bartolomeo's Challenge	On the table next to the Code Wheels

A rare one-note mystery. You'll find a few more when you solve this puzzle's counterpart in the A Game Of Wits side quest.

CHILD'S PLAY MYSTERY GUIDE

How To Start The Child's Play Mystery

This mystery kicks of in the Village in Sukhothai, an in fact, the entire mystery can be solved without leaving the village. From the fast travel sign, head up the stairs and continue straight across the boardwalk. When you see a staircase going down into the water on your right, turn around. You'll see a bottle at the bottom of the stairs floating in the water.

Pick up the bottle and break it by throwing it on the ground. We recommend walking back up the stairs and smashing it on the floor rather than breaking it in the water where the contents may be difficult to see. A note called First Bottle Message will be on the ground. Pick it up to start this mystery.

How To Solve The Child's Play Mystery

This mystery has Indy following a series of clues hidden in glass bottles all around the village. Each note has a compass pointing towards the next and a clue that directs you where to look for the next one. The First Bottle Message says "Follow the banners to the northern shrine. There is a clue in the tree next to the hut."

165

❖ First Bottle Message

From where you find the first bottle, head up the stairs and turn left. You'll see a path that leads between the buildings into an open area behind the village. Walk past the rice farms and head towards the hut mentioned in the note. It's a small, open building with two people inside conversing about thieving monkeys.

On the right side of the hut is a slanted tree. Look up in the branches, and you'll see an interact icon on a bottle. Throw your whip at the bottle to grab it out of the tree, then smash the bottle to get to the note inside.

❖ Second Bottle Message

The second bottle message says, "Walk east and find the tallest bridge. Another clue hides underneath." Head back the way you came, leaving the rice fields, and you should see the tallest bridge up the stairs to your left.

Jump off the bridge on the left side. Swim forwards, and when you find solid ground, you should see a boulder with a glass bottle sitting neatly on top of it.

❖ *Third Bottle Message*

The last bottle message says, "Walk south to the village gate. Find the boulder where the King sits on his throne." From here swim under the bridge and turn left. You'll see the south village gate straight ahead, so swim towards it.

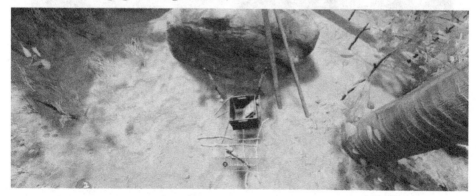

When you reach the gate walk around it to the right and you'll see the boulder straight ahead. Underneath the boulder is a small box with two items inside. The

167

first is an adventure book called Jumbo Shove, the second is the Phra Ruang Statuette. Picking up this figurine will complete the Child's Play mystery.

All Mystery Note Locations For Secret Of Secrets

Note	Location
First Bottle Message	At the bottom of a set of stairs in the village, floating in the water.
Second Bottle Message	In a year next to a hut near the northern shrine.
Third Bottle Message	Under the tallest bridge sitting on a boulder.
Phra Ruang Statuette	Next to a boulder past the south gate.

Each message is required to find the next one, so you won't have any trouble finding these notes as you progress through the quest.

FATHER AND SON MYSTERY GUIDE

How To Find The Clues

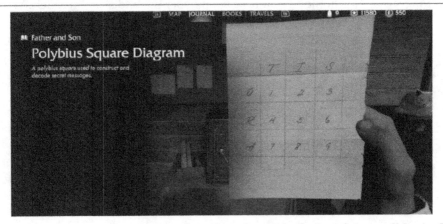

Ignore the dog sleeping and the cat meowing, they actually don't have anything to do with the puzzle. You can't even pet them!

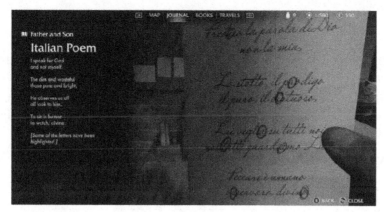

You'll find two clues in the main room, each one in a drawer of a desk in the attic you're in.

One of the notes is a Polybius Square Diagram showing nine numbers in a grid with six letters. The other note is a poem in Italian that has eight of the letters circled in red.

The Mystery in your journal says you need to find six notes for the Father and Son puzzle. However, you only need the two in the room. There's no need to keep searching.

Father And Son Mystery Safe Code

To solve the puzzle and get the safe code, you need to note down the eight letters that are circled in pairs, and then see what number corresponds to those two letters on the Polybius Square note. The letters and numbers are:

Pair of Letters	Number
I + R	5
I + A	8
T + A	7
S + O	3

169

As much as the final letter looks like an "A", it is actually an "O". The handwriting isn't the best, and that's what you may be stuck on.

Therefore, the code you need for the safe in the Father and Son Mystery is 5873. Enter that and the door will open. You'll then be able to grab the four remaining case notes you were missing and the Mystery will be completed.

MONKEY BUSINESS MYSTERY GUIDE

How To Start The Monkey Business Mystery

You will begin this quest by fast-traveling to the Secret Armory Entrance.

If you haven't unlocked this fast travel sign, you can get here by sailing south from the Wat Mahathat East entrance. The dock you're looking for is on the southeast side of the biggest island in the middle of the map. You'll know you're in the right place when you see a big chainlink fence.

Head towards the fence and crawl through the opening to get into the secret armory. Straight ahead is a big two-story tent - that's where you're headed. The safest route there is to take a left through the broken stone wall and approach the tent from the side. Head to the second floor and take out the enemy here to give yourself the freedom to explore.

If you've already found the Royal Army Outfit in Voss's camp, exploring this restricted area is much easier.

Take a picture of the Monkey Warning on the corkboard in the corner of the room to begin the quest. Then pick up Francesco's Note off of the desk next to the board to learn about the missing keys.

Finally, examine the Keyring Note on the wall next to the door. Now you have everything you need to solve this mystery.

The Monkey Warning is posted all around the big island, so there's a chance you'll have found it somewhere else already.

Where To Find The Monkeys And Equipment Room Key

Luckily, those naughty monkeys haven't gone too far. Leave the tent and go down the stairs. When you look out at the camp, you should see a guard tower in the distance; head in that direction.

Go down the stairs next to the guard tower and you'll see a truck. On the other side of the truck is a narrow path through the brush. Follow that path until you emerge on the other side.

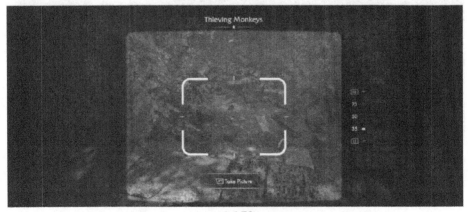

Hang a right and head towards the broken staircase. Use it to jump over the water on the other side, otherwise you'll have to slowly trudge through the mud. Climb up on the brick foundation and turn left. You should see a monkey wearing a Royal Guard helmet.

The monkeys will scatter as you approach, allowing you to grab the Equipment Room Key off the ground. Now head back to the big two-story tent and open the door to the equipment room.

Your prize for completing this mystery is the adventure book Slugger 2. Make sure you explore the room to pick up as much Nazi cash as you can find.

Monkey Business Note Locations

Monkey Warning	On the corkboard on the second floor of the big tent in the Secret Armory.
Francesco's Note	On the table next to the corkboard on the second floor of the big tent in the Secret Armory.
Keyring Note	On the wall next to the door on the second floor of the big tent in the Secret Armory.

All three notes are located in the same room, so you shouldn't have any problem completing your note collection in this quest.

A GAME OF WITS WALKTHROUGH

How To Start A Game Of Wits Mystery

In the back corner of Voss's Camp, near where you find the Royal Army Uniform, is a big green tent that represents housing the Nazi's living quarters. To begin this mystery, you'll need to make your way to the second floor using the staircase behind the tent. There you'll find a table with a board game and two notes.

Behind the table is a safe. To complete this mystery, you'll need to solve the puzzle using the notes and then input a four-digit code into the safe.

There are a few enemies patrolling this area. Either take them out or put on the Royal Army Uniform to avoid being detected while you solve this puzzle.

Pick up Lorenzo's Challenge and Mak-Yek Rules on the table to start this mystery.

This room also contains a footlocker filled with gold, a medicine bottle, and the comic book Tales of the Dread #5.

How To Solve The Mak-Yek Puzzle

As Lorenzo's Challenge explains, the goal of the puzzle is to capture all of the red pieces by moving only four blue pieces exactly once. The Mak-Yek Rules state that you can move a piece in a straight line, horizontally or vertically, until it runs into another piece. To capture a red piece, you need to surround it with two blue pieces. If multiple red pieces form a row or column, you can capture all of them by moving blue pieces to both ends.

If you flip the Mak-Yek Rules over, you'll find one additional rule written on the back of the page. If you move a blue piece in between two red pieces that are one square apart, you will capture both of them. This is called an intervention capture, and it's an essential rule to understand in order to solve the puzzle.

To open the safe, you just need to take the number from the row each blue piece moves to, in order. Every time you move a piece, write down the row it moves to, and once you've moved all four pieces, you'll have your four-digit code.

You can't actually move the piece on the Mak-Yek board unfortunately, so you'll just have to visualize each piece moving in order.

Mak-Yek Puzzle Solution

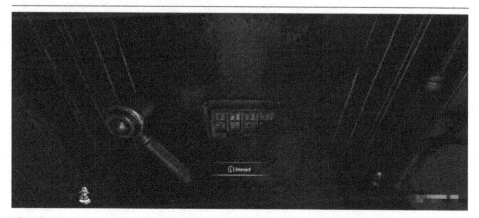

The first move you need to make is sliding the blue piece from F1 up to F3. This captures both of the red pieces on E3 and G3. The first digit of the code is 3.

The next move is to slide the blue piece from H1 to D1, capturing the red piece from C1, with the second digit of the code being 1.

Next, move B1 up to B8, this captures all of the red pieces on the top row and gives you the third digit to the code, 8.

Finally, slide the piece on F8 down to F6, which captures the final two red pieces on F5 and F4, and gives you the final digit of the code, 6.

Turn around to the safe behind the table and enter the code 3186. The door will swing open and reveal your cash prize. Congratulations, you've completed A Game of Wits!

◦   *All Mystery Note Locations For Secret Of Secrets*

Note	Location
Lorenzo's Challenge	On the table on the second floor of the green tent in Voss's Camp
Mak-Yek Rules	Underneath Lorenzo's Challenge on the same table in the green tent, second floor

These are unmissable notes since you'll need both of them to solve the puzzle. There are no notes inside the safe, just a pile of Nazi gold.

PUZZLE GUIDE

SACRED WOUNDS PUZZLE GUIDE

How To Get The Wine Bottle

The theme of the puzzle is the Sacred Wounds - those suffered by Christ on the cross As such, to start the challenge you'll need sacramental wine, which represents blood. This can be gotten from Antonio once you bring him four photographs of the Strange Inscriptions around the Vatican.

Tip: You can use the map to find Inscriptions as long as you're tracking the Secret Of Giants quest.

When you bring four photos to Antonio, place them on his desk and use the magnifying glass to highlight the gold images. Keep going as Indy and Antonio piece together the mystery. After you translate the text on the final inscription, Antonio will give you the wine.

How To Enter The Vatican Sewers

Leave the library and go east toward the Vatican Post Office, where you got the camera. Your destination, the Tower of Nicholas the Fifth, is the round building across the street. There is a captain patrolling in front of the main entrance, who can see through your disguise, so be careful getting into the building.

Once you're in, go to the sunlit chapel at the rear. Take a picture of the relief on the wall, then pour the wine into the basin in front of the altar. The relief of St. George will push out from the wall, allowing you to rotate it.

Turn the relief 180 degrees so that St. George is above the Dragon, and the wall will recede, allowing you into the catacombs.

❖ Inside The Tunnels

Take the torch just inside the entrance and use the candle on the altar to light it. Before you go down, use the stairs to climb up the tower, jumping to clear the gaps. A lost relic is at the top, waiting to be collected.

Continue downward until you come to a room with torches on the wall to light. Do so, then place your torch in the remaining sconce. This will unlock the door, letting you enter the Sacred Wounds puzzle room.

How To Solve The Sacred Wounds Puzzle

Directly ahead of you is an image of the Crucifixion, with levers located near each of the five wounds. Pour wine into the central basin to activate the levers and start the puzzle. You need to find the correct position for each lever. On either side of the main mechanism are two murals, each with basins in front of them. Pouring wine into each mural's basin will reveal a Roman numeral. For the left mural, you'll need to move a fallen bust off of the basin first.

On each mural, a part of Christ's body is highlighted by a halo; match the Roman numeral to the highlighted hand, foot, or chest, to determine which position the associated lever needs to be in.

There are two more murals in the room to the left, and one in the room to the right. The room to the left can be entered normally, but the door will slam shut behind you Pick up an iron rod and smash through the wall next to the statue of Longinus to get back to the main room.

The room on the right is closed, but you can squeeze through a crack in the wall to the right of the door, then open it from the other side.

Don't forget to take pictures of each of the murals as you go for extra Adventure Points.

❖ Sacred Wounds Puzzle Solution

Wound	Mural	Roman Numeral
Right Hand	Holy Chalice	II (2)
Left Hand	Body Of Christ	II (2)
Chest	Spear Of Longinus	III (3)
Right Foot	Anointment Of Jesus	IV (4)
Left Foot	Walking On Water	III (3)

Note: Left and right are from the viewer's perspective.

Once all five levers are correctly set, the wall will open, allowing you into the sewers to continue your search.

Where Is The Fountain Of Confession?

The easiest way to get to the Fountain of Confession is to take the west exit from the Belvedere Courtyards, the main plaza in Vatican City. You'll find yourself near the checkpoint with the troop inspection south of the barracks where you rescued Sidney earlier.

You can't start the Fountain puzzle until you've met Gina and the German zeppelin has arrived in the Vatican, so there's no need to rush here. You'll encounter Gina after emerging from the Tomb of the Warrior Giant under the Tower of Nicholas the Fifth.

Go up the hill to the left of the inspection line, taking care to avoid being noticed by the captain. Follow the garden path, and you'll see the Fountain of Confession looming in front of you. Don't forget to take a picture of the Fountain itself, plus the inscriptions on either side of it.

How To Turn The Dragons At The Fountain Of Confession

Start by checking the lockbox to the left and taking the Fountain Gate Key inside. This will let you open the door to the left of the Fountain. Before you do, though, check the backs of the truck parked nearby for some extra money; you can use a melee weapon like a hammer to smash the padlocks on the cash box.

Inside the Fountain, use your whip to climb and swing to the window by the roof. This will bring you to the dragon statues on the turrets above the inscriptions.

You need to rotate the statues so that they are facing one another. Start by swinging across to the Dark Dragon Statue. Rotate its outstretched claw to activate a lever which you can use to turn the statue until it's facing the center of the Fountain.,

Swing back to the Light Dragon Statue; its claw is missing. If you look over the edge of the construction scaffolding, you'll see the claw below; climb down to pick it up and trigger a cutscene, after which you can climb back up to reattach it.

Once both statues are facing inward, three statues will appear at the center of the Fountain of Confession, letting you begin the next section of the puzzle.

Each new section of sculpture that gets revealed can be photographed for bonus Adventure Points.

How To Solve The Baptism Puzzle At The Fountain Of Confession

Climb back down and help Gina push the lever that emerged from the Fountain all the way to the left. This will reveal a baptism scene that you need to interact with.

Start by pushing the child statue on the left as far to the right as it will go; the child should be lined up with the sconce behind it.

Next, use the whip to pull the chain above the priest statue on the right. This will fill the baptismal vessel with water. Push the priest statue to the left until the water spills onto the child statue.

If done correctly, the mechanism will rotate back to the angel statues, and one will recede, indicating that you've made progress. Return to the main lever and push it to the right to start the next puzzle.

How To Solve The Ark Of Bulrushes Puzzle

The Ark of Bulrushes is the hardest of the puzzles in this challenge; while it's simple in premise, a single mistake can force you to backtrack a lot. No doubt Indy's had his fill of Arks by this point, too.

The boat starts partially in the puzzle; you need to reset the mechanism by using the whip to pull the left chain before you do anything else.

You can rotate the three wheels by grabbing the stones and moving them, but the planks in the grooves can cause multiple wheels to turn at once. The aim is to get both planks to fall safely into the crevasse at the bottom, while at the same time setting up a clear path across the center from left to right for the boat to travel.

Start by getting one plank into the bottom crevasse and permanently out of the way. From there, get the other plank into the middle groove of the center disk so that it doesn't overlap with any others, then turn it sideways so that it won't move while you're getting the others into position.

Move the middle and outer disks so that they form a "T" shape; once they're in position, rotate the center disk to drop the plank, then move it to complete the T. If all goes well, you'll have created a path for the boat.

Once the path is clear, use the whip to pull the right-hand chain and set the boat in motion. If the puzzle is set incorrectly and the boat gets stuck, pull the left chain again to reset it.

If the boat makes it to the right side, the angel statues will return, and the second one will recede. Push the center statue through the iron gate to open the way to the hidden monastery, and the dangers that lie within.

SILVER PATH TRIAL PUZZLE GUIDE

How To Start Silver Trial

From the moment you enter the trial, swing across the flames with your whip to the other end of the room. You'll see a stone tablet behind a closed door.

Head back to the middle of the room, head right and right again, and you'll see another stone tablet being clutched by a skeleton on the floor. Grab it from him.

Go back to the main room and place the tablet on the pedestal in the centre of it. Fire will then come from the bottom of the room and the original door you couldn't get past will now be open, so swing across and grab the tablet from the pedestal there.

Whatever you do, do not fall into the fire. You'll have to repeat what you just did if you do.

How To Escape The Fire

Once you've done that, more fire will start so you'll need to give the tablet you just grabbed to Gina, who's behind the bars to your side. She'll be shouting at you to give her the tablet.

She'll take the tablet to the pedestal on the other side of the room. When you try to swing across again, the grapple point will break and you'll have to climb around to your left, up a piece of the room that's just collapsed.

Once you reach the middle part of the room, drop down and swing across to the far end where Gina is waiting for you. Grab the tablet from her and place it on the pedestal. That will open the door, so swing across to the middle and run out of the chamber.

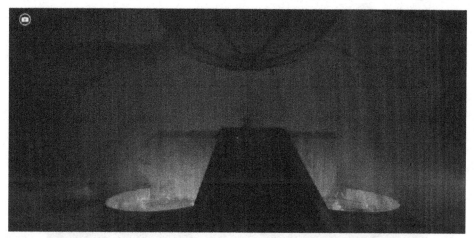

That's the main part of the trial completed, but you now need to run to the middle of the structure in front of you and grab the chain, rotating the statues until they're all as high as they'll go.

You can then leave the chamber, using your whip to pull down water to solidify the key you need to open the door.

You can use the key in the door now or wait until you have both of them after completing the other trial.

GOLD PATH TRIAL PUZZLE GUIDE

Gold Path Trial Puzzle Walkthrough

Once you enter the gold trial chamber, you'll see a lever at the far end. You can walk to it, but interacting with it won't do anything as the door remains locked until you solve the puzzle.

You can walk over any part of the arena that's not actively on fire. Steam and sparks won't hurt you, so don't worry about that.

From the lever, head left and go behind the bars where you'll find some chains you can pull. Pull those chains until the towers that move in the main chamber go over the fire sections and light up brightly.

How To Move Hidden Chains

Once you've done those two towers, head back to the entrance of the trial, and you'll spot a whip grapple point just by the side of the main area. Whip up to that and climb onto the nearest tower, which you previously lit.

Indy will then ask Gina for help moving the tower to where you need it to be to continue climbing. That'll allow you to whip onto another grapple point and pull yourself up into a broken entrance way above the other side of the clamber.

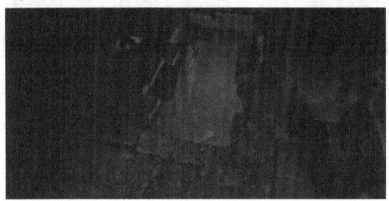

Drop down into there through the hole and you'll be behind the bars you previously couldn't reach due to a locked door. Pull the chains in there too to light up the floor beneath them, then head back to the other side after opening the door with the chain.

You'll need to head back to the chains you moved first to move the tower Gina moved back to where it needs to be.

With all towers now lit, you'll be able to open the main door using the lever. In the next chamber, pull the chain to rotate the statues and activate the forge.

After leaving that room, you can then use your whip pull ability to solidify the metal and grab the key to open the door that ends both trials. You can either put the key in the door now or wait until you've completed both of the trials.

How to Solve the Exhibit puzzle

After the scene with the giant, you are tasked with restoring order to a shattered museum display. Scattered artifacts lie amidst the debris and your job is to to place them back in their correct positions. Examine each artifact carefully; their unique shapes and markings offer clues to their proper placement but most important are the comments by Indiana and Brody.

Whenever you pick up an artifact, Indiana and Brody will comment about the origin of the artifacts. The flags next to the display cases can be used to identify the correct location for each artifact. Match the artifact's origin (as indicated by Indiana and Brody's comments) to the corresponding flag on the display case. If you want to try and solve the puzzle by yourself, you can stop reading, otherwise, keep reading for the solution.

❖ *Where to Place the Bastet Statue*

First, pick up the Bastet Statue from the floor.

As mentioned by Indiana, the Bastet Statue is Ancient Egyptian, and you can see one of the display cases contains the flag of the Kingdom of Egypt, a green background with a white half moon and three stars. The first picture on the back is an artwork of Bastet, a figure with a feline cat's holding an ankh and a staff, and the Eye of Horus at the top.

185

❖ Where to Place the Terracotta Relief

First, pick up the Terracotta Relief from the floor, which is right next to where you found the Bastet Statue.

Indiana will comment that the Terracotta is Babylonian, out of Iraq. Look for a display case with the flag of the Kingdom of Iraq. Three horizontal stripes, black white and green and a red trapezoid on the left with two white seven-pointed stars.

❖ Where to Place the Ivory Case

Upon picking it up, Indiana mentions Ugaritic letters from the Ivory Case. Ugarit was an ancient port city in northern Syria. It was discovered just a few years before the current in-game year.

One of the display cases at the end of the row contains a Syrian flag, three horizontal stripes, green, white and black with three red stars in the middle. At the back of the display, you can find a cuneiform chart and the picture of an old stone tablet.

Place the Ivory Case and continue.

❖ Where to Place the Funerary Mask

Pick up the Funerary Mask from the floor and listen to Indiana's comments.

The only hint you get is that it's solid gold. Luckily, there's a display case with images of rings and belts made of gold with a Syrian flag.

Made in the USA
Monee, IL
14 December 2024

73859492R00105